The Secret Language of Birthdays - February Personality Insights

Birthdays Profiles, Volume 2

Daniel Sanjurjo

Published by Daniel Sanjurjo, 2023.

Published

By Daniel Sanjurjo, 2024.
While every precaution has been taken in the preparation of this book, the publisher assumes no responsibility for errors or omissions, or for damages resulting from the use of the information contained herein.
The Secret Language of Birthdays Profiles - January Personality Insights
First edition. December 30, 2023.
Copyright © 2024 Daniel Sanjurjo.
Written by Daniel Sanjurjo.

Table of Contents

Introduction 1

A Journey Through February Birthdays 3

The Secret Language Unveiled: 7

The Astrological Sign of February - Aquarius ♒ 9

The Astrological Sign of February - Pisces ♓ 12

Astrological Profile for Those Born on February 1 15

Astrological Profile for Those Born on February 2 17

Astrological Profile for Those Born on February 3 19

Astrological Profile for Those Born on February 4 21

Astrological Profile for Those Born on February 5 23

Astrological Profile for Those Born on February 6 25

Astrological Profile for Those Born on February 7 27

Astrological Profile for Those Born on February 8 29

Astrological Profile for Those Born on February 9 31

Astrological Profile for Those Born on February 10 33

Astrological Profile for Those Born on February 11 35

Astrological Profile for Those Born on February 12 37

Astrological Profile for Those Born on February 13 39

Astrological Profile for Those Born on February 14 41

Astrological Profile for Those Born on February 15 43

Astrological Profile for Those Born on February 16 45

Astrological Profile for Those Born on February 17 47

Astrological Profile for Those Born on February 18 49

Astrological Profile for Those Born on February 19 51

Astrological Profile for Those Born on February 20 53

Astrological Profile for Those Born on February 21st: 55

Astrological Profile for Those Born on February 22 57

Astrological Profile for Those Born on February 23 59

Astrological Profile for Those Born on February 24 61

Astrological Profile for Those Born on February 25 63

Astrological Profile for Those Born on February 26 65

Astrological Profile for Those Born on February 27 67

Astrological Profile for Those Born on February 28 69

Astrological Profile for Those Born on February 29 71

Insights into Aquarius and Pisces Compatibility 73

Book Overview: "The Secret Language of Birthdays" 76

How to Read a Birth Chart: Astrology for Beginners? 79

Brief Overview of Astrology and Its Significance..........................82

Significance in Understanding Personalities: 83

Basic Astrological Concepts...84

Birth Chart Interpretation 86

Lunar Guidance: Moon's Secrets in Your Birth Chart 89

Finding the Right Astrology Software 96

Zodiac Signs and Characteristics 97

Planetary Influences on Personality...99

Astrological Elements and Modalities 102

Numerology Integration 104

Compatibility and Relationships.. 106

Tips for Relationship Enhancement: 108

Astrological Transits and Life Events.. 109

Practical Applications of Astrological Insights 111

Astrological Case Studies... 113

Explore the science behind birthdays.. 118

Unique Traditions and Festivities 121

February Birthday Celebrations: Unleash the Inner Flame!...... 123

February Birthdays:.. 125

Conclusion: Embrace the Cosmic Tapestry of Self-Discovery.. 127

Contact the astrologer 130

About the Author.. 134

Introduction

Welcome to "The Secret Language of Birthdays - February Profiles: Personality Insights"

Embark on an extraordinary voyage through the cosmic corridors of February with "The Secret Language of Birthdays - February Profiles: Personality Insights." In this celestial compendium, we unravel the enigmatic language of the stars, focusing our cosmic lens specifically on the unique individuals born on each day of this enchanting month.

What Awaits You:

1. Daily Astrological Portraits:

• Immerse yourself in daily astrological profiles, crafted with precision and tailored to illuminate the distinct personality traits of those born in February.

2. Numerological Revelations:

• Delve into the secrets of numerology, uncovering the hidden numerical codes that weave through the fabric of each February day, offering profound insights into individual life paths.

3. Personalized Personality Insights:

• Navigate the intricate landscapes of personality with detailed insights into the strengths, tendencies, and potential life paths of individuals born on every day of February.

4. Relationship Alchemy:

• Unlock the secrets of interpersonal dynamics as we explore how the cosmic energies of February influence relationships, friendships, and partnerships.

5. Celestial Transits and Life Events:

• Navigate the cosmic currents with a spotlight on planetary transits, understanding how celestial movements shape significant life events during each day of February.

6. Practical Cosmic Wisdom:

• Harness the power of astrological wisdom in your daily life. From decision-making to time management, discover practical applications that align your actions with the cosmic energies of February.

7. Real-Life Cosmic Chronicles:

• Immerse yourself in captivating case studies, real-life narratives that unfold the cosmic influence on individuals born on each day of February.

A Journey Through February Birthdays

February, the second month of the year, has a rich history and significance in various cultures and calendars. Let's delve into the origins and explore its multifaceted importance.

1. **Roman Roots:** In the ancient Roman calendar, February was originally the last month of the year. It had 28 days, except during leap years when an extra day was added. The name "February" is believed to derive from the Latin word "februum," meaning purification, as it was a time for cleansing rituals.

2. **Februa Festival:** The Romans celebrated the Februa festival during this month, a period of purification and atonement. This festival contributed to the association of February with cleansing and renewal.

3. **Transition in Calendars:** With the adoption of the Julian calendar by Julius Caesar in 45 BCE, February retained its place as the second month. The Gregorian calendar, introduced by Pope Gregory XIII in 1582 to align the calendar year with the solar year, further refined the leap year rules.

4. **Celebrations in Honor of Deities:** In ancient Rome, February was dedicated to the deities Juno and Lupercus. Juno was the goddess of marriage and women, and Lupercus was associated with shepherds and fertility. The Lupercalia festival, held in mid-February, involved rituals of purification and fertility.

5. **Candlemas and Groundhog Day:** February 2nd marks Candlemas, a Christian festival commemorating the presentation of Jesus at the Temple. Additionally, Groundhog Day, with its roots in European weather lore, falls on this

date, symbolizing the midpoint between the winter solstice and the spring equinox.

6. **Chinese New Year:** In the lunar-based Chinese calendar, February hosts the celebration of the Chinese New Year. This vibrant festival, also known as the Spring Festival, marks the beginning of the lunar new year and is a time for family reunions, feasts, and cultural festivities.

7. **Birthstone and Birth Flower:** Amethyst, a purple gemstone symbolizing clarity and inner strength, is the birthstone for February. Additionally, the violet is the birth flower, representing modesty and faithfulness.

8. **Modern Traditions:** In contemporary times, February is celebrated with Valentine's Day on the 14th, a day dedicated to love and affection. It has become a month associated with matters of the heart and expressions of love.

9. **Historical Birthdays:** Some notable historical figures born in February include Abraham Lincoln, George Washington, Charles Darwin, and Rosa Parks, contributing to the month's significance in the annals of history.

Cultural Perspectives:

• Lappland's Hibernation Games: In Finland's frosty Lapland, February hosts the quirky Hibernation Games. This playful celebration, featuring wife-carrying and reindeer racing, brings a spirited energy to February birthdays in the region.

• Brazilian Carnival: For those born under the fiery sign of Carnival, February explodes with vibrant costumes, pulsating music, and unbridled revelry. It's a time of letting loose and embracing life's joyful chaos, perfectly mirroring the energetic spirit of February birthdays.

• Setsubun in Japan: This February festival involves throwing roasted soybeans to ward off evil spirits and usher in good luck. For

Japanese February babies, it signifies resilience and the power of positive action, shaping their personal journeys.

Folklore and Superstitions:

● Strong and Adaptable: Many believe February babies, forged in the coldest months, develop resilience, independence, and the ability to thrive in challenging conditions. This adds a touch of strength and determination to their birth month.

● Amethyst's Magic: February's birthstone, the amethyst, is said to promote peace, protection, and inner strength. Wearing or owning amethyst can empower February birthdays, aligning them with the stone's symbolic qualities.

● Midwinter Traditions: In some cultures, February marks the halfway point between winter solstice and spring equinox. This signifies hope, anticipation, and the gradual return of light, resonating with the potential and growth inherent in February birthdays.

Celebrating Your February Spark:

Understanding the unique history and cultural significance of February birthdays can enrich your personal narrative. Embrace the cleansing spirit of its ancient rituals, draw inspiration from vibrant cultural celebrations, and connect with the strength and resilience associated with the month. As a February baby, you are part of a global tapestry woven with history, folklore, and the promise of spring's renewal. Celebrate your special birth month with pride, knowing that its frosty depths hold a hidden warmth and endless possibilities.

So, dear February birthday, remember, yours is not just a month of cold winds and shorter days. It's a time of ancient blessings, vibrant celebrations, and hidden strengths waiting to be unleashed. Embrace your unique birth month and let its magic guide you on a journey of growth, resilience, and joyful beginnings.

In conclusion, February's history is woven with threads of ancient Roman rituals, Christian traditions, and diverse cultural celebrations. Its place in various calendars and its associations with purification, fertility, and love make it a month of layered significance across the ages.

The Secret Language Unveiled:

February's cosmic symphony is rich with individual notes, each day a unique chord resonating with distinct energies. As we uncover the secret language of birthdays, let this book be your guide—a portal to self-discovery, cosmic wisdom, and a deeper understanding of the intricate dance between the stars and those born in the month of February. Your cosmic journey begins here.

In February, we've got a cosmic tag team of two zodiac signs: Aquarius and Pisces.

1. **Aquarius (January 20 - February 18):**

   • **Who They Are:** Imagine the friend who's always one step ahead, full of fresh ideas and a strong sense of justice.

   • **What to Expect:** Aquarians are the trailblazers, known for their independence, love of all things innovative, and a big heart for making the world a better place.

2. **Pisces (February 19 - March 20):**

   • **Meet the Dreamer:** As we move further into February, we step into Pisces territory.

   • **Their Vibe:** Picture the artist who lives in the world of dreams, with a heart that feels deeply and a mind that's creatively charged.

   • **Key Traits:** Pisceans bring a tidal wave of emotion, intuition that's on point, and a touch of magic to everything they do.

So, in February, it's like having a cosmic mixtape playing. First, the Aquarians get us grooving with their forward-thinking beats. Then, the Pisceans take the stage, bringing a soulful melody of emotions and imagination. People born in February get the best of both worlds, creating a symphony of unique traits influenced by these cosmic dance partners.

The Astrological Sign of February - Aquarius ♒

Aquarius (January 20 - February 18)

Let's dive into the cosmic energies that shape the personalities of those born in the early part of February under the influence of Aquarius.

Who Are Aquarians?

1. Innovative Thinkers:

- Aquarians are the forward-thinkers of the zodiac, always one step ahead with original ideas.

- They thrive on intellectual challenges and are known for their inventive solutions to problems.

2. Humanitarians at Heart:

- With a strong sense of justice and equality, Aquarians are often driven by a desire to make the world a better place.

- They champion social causes and are drawn to humanitarian efforts.

3. Independent Souls:

- Independence is a core trait of Aquarians; they value their freedom and resist conformity.

- They are unafraid to march to the beat of their own drum and embrace their individuality.

Key Traits of Aquarius

1. Intellectual Prowess:

- Aquarians are intellectually curious, constantly seeking knowledge and new perspectives.

- Their analytical minds make them adept problem-solvers and great contributors to group discussions.

2. Open-Minded Visionaries:

- Open-mindedness is a hallmark of Aquarians; they are willing to explore unconventional ideas and challenge the status quo.

- Their visionary outlook often leads to groundbreaking insights and progressive viewpoints.

3. Socially Connected:

- Despite their independent nature, Aquarians value social connections and thrive in group settings.

- They build a diverse network of friends and acquaintances, enjoying the exchange of ideas and experiences.

Ruled by Uranus
1. Uranus, the Rebel:

- Aquarius is ruled by Uranus, the planet associated with innovation and sudden change.

- This influence adds a touch of rebellion to Aquarian energy, fueling their desire for transformation and societal progress.

2. Electric Energy:

• The electrifying energy of Uranus contributes to Aquarius' ability to shake things up and introduce a spark of inspiration wherever they go.

In the cosmic tapestry of February, Aquarius sets the stage with its unique blend of intellect, innovation, and a deep commitment to making a positive impact on the world. Those born under the sign of Aquarius bring a breath of fresh air to the zodiac, reminding us to embrace change, celebrate individuality, and always look to the future.

The Astrological Sign of February - Pisces ♓

Pisces (February 19 - March 20)

Welcome to the ethereal realm of Pisces, the astrological sign that graces the celestial stage during the enchanting month of February. Symbolized by the two fish swimming in opposite directions, Pisces encapsulates a world of imagination, emotion, and intuition.

Characteristics of Pisces Individuals

1. Emotional Depth:

- Pisceans are known for their profound emotional sensitivity and empathy.

- They navigate the currents of emotions with a deep understanding of both their own feelings and those of others.

2. Imaginative Souls:

- Ruled by Neptune, the planet of dreams and inspiration, Pisceans possess a rich imagination.

- This imaginative prowess often translates into creative pursuits, making them artists, poets, or dreamers.

3. Intuitive Wisdom:

- Gifted with an innate intuition, Pisces individuals can tap into the unseen and trust their gut feelings.

- This intuitive wisdom guides them in navigating life's complexities with a heightened sense of perception.

4. Adaptive Nature:

• Pisceans are adaptable and can flow effortlessly in various situations.

• Their mutable quality allows them to adjust to changing circumstances, making them versatile individuals.

Influences of Neptune, Ruling Planet of Pisces
1. Spiritual Connection:

• Neptune, the ruler of Pisces, brings a spiritual dimension to their personality.

• Pisceans often seek a deeper connection to the mystical and may find solace in spiritual practices.

2. Artistic Expression:

• Neptune's influence enhances the artistic inclination of Pisceans.

• Whether through visual arts, music, or other creative outlets, they find expression in the ethereal and the imaginative.

Overview of Water Element
1. Emotional Fluidity:

• As a water sign, Pisces is deeply connected to emotions and the subconscious.

• Their emotional fluidity allows them to navigate the ever-changing tides of life with grace.

2. Intuitive Connection:

• The water element enhances Pisces' intuitive nature, fostering a strong connection to the unseen and the mystical.

In the cosmic ballet of astrology, Pisces in February offers a glimpse into a world where emotions, creativity, and intuition intertwine, creating individuals with a unique and magical essence. As we journey deeper into the month, let the watery embrace of Pisces guide us through the cosmic currents of self-discovery and understanding.

Astrological Profile for Those Born on February 1

If February 1 is your birthdate, your star sign is Aquarius, and your ruling planets are Uranus and the Sun. Let's explore the unique traits and potential destiny written in the cosmic script of your birth.

Aquarius Essence

• **Creative Potential:** You possess extraordinary creative potential and charisma, elevating your presence by selecting impeccable attire to make a lasting impression.

• **Leadership Aura:** A natural-born leader, people look up to you. Be mindful not to misuse the respect and authority vested in you.

• **Solar Vibration:** The Solar vibration of the number 1 imparts an unusual streak to your nature. Quick-witted, daring, and highly strung, you may exhibit eccentric tendencies, making creative fields with a dramatic flair ideal for your expression.

Ambitions and Career

If born on February 1, ambition courses through your veins. The inclination to seek roles allowing autonomy is strong. Some may step out of their comfort zones, but it's essential to balance ambition with realistic expectations.

Influences of Uranus

• **Intuition and Compassion:** Under the influence of Uranus, your intuition is heightened, and a desire to contribute to the common good guides your actions.

• **Compassion in Action:** Compassionate and driven by the welfare of others, be cautious not to pursue ideas that may inadvertently harm others.

Personal Traits and Challenges

• **Driven and Passionate:** You are driven, passionate, and deeply committed to your loved ones.

• **Imaginative Excellence:** Highly imaginative, you have the potential to excel in various professions.

• **Time Management:** Manage time wisely to avoid dissatisfaction or unhappiness. Balancing obligations is crucial.

Lucky Attributes

• **Colors:** Yellow and gold are your lucky colors.

• **Gem:** Ruby is your lucky gem.

• **Days of the Week:** Sunday, Monday, and Thursday are favorable for you.

• **Numbers:** Your lucky numbers are 1, 10, 19, 28, 37, 46, 55, 64, 73, and 82.

Famous Birthdays

Notable personalities born on February 1 include John Ford, Clark Gable, Lisa-Marie Presley, Brandon Lee, Sherilyn Fenn, Brian Krause, and Jarrett Lennon.

In the cosmic dance of astrology, your birth on February 1 unfolds a story of leadership, creativity, and compassionate action. May your journey be as vibrant as the colors you hold dear and as precious as the gem that adorns your cosmic identity.

Astrological Profile for Those Born on February 2

If February 2 is your birthdate, your star sign is Aquarius, and your ruling planets are Uranus and the Moon. Let's delve into the unique characteristics and cosmic influences that shape your personality.

Aquarius Essence

• **Expressive Love:** You express love by sharing your emotions, though you may exhibit moodiness. Your desire to be universally liked is apparent, but be cautious not to compromise your authenticity for approval.

• **Imagination and Idealism:** High on imagination and idealism, you are a dreamer who finds joy in fantasizing about possibilities.

• **Influence of the Moon:** Governed by the Moon, your emotional nature experiences sudden and abrupt changes. Relationships, especially with women, may undergo fluctuations due to the influence of the spontaneous Uranus.

Emotional Dynamics

• **Erratic Behavior:** Your erratic behavior can lead to both favorable and challenging circumstances, especially in relationships.

• **Psychic Development:** Utilize your foresight wisely for careful life planning. This can lead to excellence in psychic development and profound spiritual insights.

• **Nature Connection:** Associate yourself with natural settings, particularly the ocean, to temper the highly strung energies within you and find satisfaction.

Career and Passion

• **Compassionate Hearts:** Individuals born on February 2 have compassionate hearts and a desire for the spotlight. They are often seen as philanthropists despite their directness.

- **Passion for the Arts:** Passion for the arts may attract them to careers in creative fields, making them appealing to employers.
- **Unusual Personality:** People born on this day may have an unusual personality, gravitating towards technology-related jobs or hobbies.

Relationships and Compatibility

- **Social Character:** Highly developed social character, but can sometimes come across as arrogant or selfish. Openness and accessibility are key to connecting with them.
- **Astrological Compatibility:** Aquarius is most compatible with Libra and may face challenges in romance with Cancer.

Numerology Insights

- **Numerical Associations:** The number 2 symbolizes kindness and gentleness, while the number 4 represents balance, completion, and realization.

Lucky Attributes

- **Lucky Colors:** Cream and white are your lucky colors.
- **Lucky Gems:** Moonstone or pearl are your lucky gems.
- **Lucky Days:** Monday, Thursday, and Sunday are favorable for you.
- **Lucky Numbers:** Your fortunate numbers are 2, 11, 20, 29, 38, 47, 56, 65, 74.

Famous Birthdays

Notable individuals born on February 2 include Havelock Ellis, James Joyce, Jascha Heifetz, Ayn Rand, Stan Gets, Farrah Fawcett, Brent Spiner, and Michael T Weiss.

As you navigate the cosmic currents of your birthdate, may your compassionate heart, innovative spirit, and artistic passion guide you towards a fulfilling and vibrant journey through life.

Astrological Profile for Those Born on February 3

If February 3 is your birthdate, your star sign is Aquarius, and your personal ruling planets are Uranus and Jupiter. Let's explore the unique characteristics and cosmic influences that shape your vibrant personality.

Aquarius Essence

• **Jovial Spirit:** Ruled by the beneficial Jupiter, you embody a jovial and exuberant spirit. High standards, integrity, and fair play define your moral and spiritual nature.

• **Empathy and Compassion:** Exhibiting empathy and compassion, you genuinely care for all people. Your executive abilities are complemented by well-balanced and sound judgment.

• **Optimism and Positivity:** A naturally optimistic and positive outlook ensures your acceptance by others. Communication fields thrive on your upbeat energy.

Personal Traits and Challenges

• **High Standards:** Striving for high standards in all areas of life, you maintain honesty in dealings and self-confidence.

• **Risk-Taking Tendency:** Be cautious of a tendency to take uncalculated risks due to your high-thinking and big planning.

Social Dynamics

• **Curious and Open-Minded:** Individuals born on February 3 are known for curiosity, open-mindedness, friendliness, and independence.

• **Active and Outgoing:** Highly active and outgoing, they navigate social situations with great timing.

Relationship Insights

• **Relationship Style:** Cancer sign associations indicate a preference for dating mysterious and imaginative individuals. While enjoying freedom, those born on February 3 may prefer shorter relationships.

- **Stability in Relationships:** Stability in relationships is achievable for those who share their passions. Fears about marriage or having children may be unfounded, as Aquarians tend to build stable relationships.

Numerology Insights

- **Numerical Associations:** Your numbers and planetary vibrations suggest a tendency to take risks, sometimes of an uncalculated nature.

Astrological Compatibility

- **Zodiac Compatibility:** Aquarians born on February 3 are likely to be most compatible with signs that align with their dynamic and social nature.

Lucky Attributes

- **Lucky Colors:** Yellow is your lucky color.

Famous Birthdays

Notable individuals born on February 3 include Havelock Ellis, James Joyce, Jascha Heifetz, Ayn Rand, Stan Gets, Farrah Fawcett, Brent Spiner, and Michael T Weiss.

May your journey through life be as vibrant as your optimistic spirit, and may the cosmic influences of Uranus and Jupiter continue to guide you towards success and fulfillment.

Astrological Profile for Those Born on February 4

If February 4 is your birthdate, your star sign is Aquarius, and your personal ruling planet is Uranus. Let's delve into the unique characteristics and cosmic influences that shape your methodical and revolutionary nature.

Aquarius Essence

- **Methodical Thinking:** Extremely methodical in thought, you possess a strong work ethic. However, it's essential to temper your opinions and consider other people's points of view.

- **Self-Criticism:** Due to your hardworking nature, there may be a tendency to exceed your physical capacity, leading to self-criticism. Balance material success with attention to your spiritual and inner life.

Planetary Influences

- **Uranus Dominance:** Completely ruled by Uranus, your birth date also carries the influence of the Dragon, specifically the North Node. Embrace these revolutionary energies for practical achievements rather than venturing into untried areas too hastily.

- **Electrical Aura:** Possessing an electrical aura, you exude magnetic energy, making a significant impact in the world. Channel this energy into constructive endeavors.

Zodiac Insights

- **Water Sign in Aquarius:** As a water sign in the second decan of Aquarius (February 1 to February 9), you exhibit a balanced blend of passion, creativity, practicality, and openness to new ideas.

Personality Traits

- **Adventurous Spirit:** Enjoying the company of others, especially those with a sense of adventure, your interests align well with fellow Aquarians, whether in politics or the arts.

• **Generosity and Spontaneity:** Uranus's influence makes you generous and spontaneous, especially with resources. Be mindful of impulsiveness and balance it with constructive actions.

Energetic Drive

• **High Energy Levels:** Highly energetic, you use your energy to accomplish various tasks. Distribute your energy constructively, taking on one project at a time to avoid overwhelm.

• **Strength in Laughter:** While keeping some thoughts to yourself enhances efficiency, make time for laughter to maintain a positive and balanced approach.

Numerology and Lucky Attributes

• **Numerical Associations:** The extreme nature of the number 4 signifies a strong desire for material success. Your lucky colors are Electric Blue, Electric White, and Multi-colors.

• **Lucky Gems:** Hessonite garnet and agate are your lucky gems.

• **Lucky Days:** Sunday and Thursday are favorable days.

• **Lucky Numbers:** 4, 13, 22, 31, 40, 49, 58, 67, 76 are your fortunate numbers.

Famous Birthdays

Notable individuals born on February 4 include Charles Lindbergh, Ida Lupino, Alice Cooper, Laura Linney, Michael Goorjian, Oscar De La Hoya, and Natalie Imbruglia.

May your methodical approach and revolutionary spirit lead you to a fulfilling and impactful journey through life.

Astrological Profile for Those Born on February 5

If February 5 is your birthdate, your star sign is Aquarius, and your personal ruling planets are Uranus and Mercury. Let's explore the dynamic blend of energies that shape your swift, curious, and inventive nature.

Aquarius Essence

• **Mercurial Zing:** Mercury adds vibrancy to your nature, making you swift, curious, and inventive. Your insatiable curiosity and love of family make you forever youthful in spirit.

• **Intellectual Aptitude:** Endowed with an agile mind, you excel in studious and intellectual pursuits. Your spontaneous insights and quick thinking contribute to effective problem-solving.

Planetary Influences

• **Uranus and Mercury Dynamics:** The combined energies of Uranus and Mercury grant you an incredible ability to absorb information. Uranus instills spontaneity, while Mercury enhances inventive, shrewd, and scientific thinking.

• **Curiosity and Industriousness:** Your nature is marked by curiosity, intuition, and industriousness. Quick grasp of ideas, correct conclusions, and good planning skills contribute to success in progressive businesses.

Personality Traits

• **Restlessness and Confidence:** While your confidence may impress others, it masks underlying insecurities. Your overconfidence may be a shield, and your intellect and daring ways can make you feel capable yet restless.

• **Urge to Assist:** Despite not being your natural instinct, you may feel an urge to assist others. Your unique ability to think quickly and abstractly can be a valuable asset in helping those around you.

Birth Chart Insights

• **Saturn and Uranus Rulership:** Governed by Saturn and Uranus, your birth chart reflects seriousness and a unique ability to bounce back. Mercury's influence indicates abstract thinking and a quest for truth.

Birthstone and Symbolism

• **Aquamarine Birthstone:** Connected to the throat chakra and Mercury, aquamarine helps express true selves, connect with water spirits, and find resolution. It aids in understanding one's mission.

Lucky Attributes

• **Lucky Color:** Green is your fortunate color.

• **Lucky Gems:** Emerald, Aquamarine, or Jade are your lucky gems.

• **Lucky Days:** Wednesdays, Fridays, and Saturdays are favorable.

• **Lucky Numbers:** 5, 14, 23, 32, 41, 50, 59, 68, 77 are your fortunate numbers.

Famous Birthdays

Notable individuals born on February 5 include J.K. Huysmans, Adlai Stevenson, William Burroughs, Red Buttons, Jennifer Jason Leigh, and Duff McKagan.

May your mercurial and dynamic nature lead you to a life filled with intellectual pursuits, meaningful connections, and spontaneous insights.

Astrological Profile for Those Born on February 6

If February 6 is your birthdate, your star sign is Aquarius, and your personal ruling planets are Uranus and Venus. Let's delve into the traits and influences that shape your agreeable personality.

Aquarian Essence

- **Agreeable Personality:** Your personality is agreeable, and you tend to maintain friendships even when they may have lost their value. Learning to let go of relationships that no longer serve you is crucial for your personal growth.

- **Attraction to Opposite Sex:** Strongly attracted to the opposite sex, you are never without admirers. This quality, influenced by Venus, the Planet of Love, signifies potential for worldly success and fulfilling personal relationships.

Venusian Influence

- **Venus Rulership:** Venus governs your birth chart, bringing forth love, sympathy, harmony, and aesthetic appreciation. While your nature is generally agreeable, there might be instances where you compromise your views to maintain friendships. Standing firm and adhering to your principles can lead to societal respect.

- **Artistic Pursuits:** With enthusiasm, charm, and wit, a career in the arts aligns well with your attributes, offering an ideal outlet for your creativity.

Personal Characteristics

- **Ambition and Self-Perception:** Ambitious yet prone to underestimating your abilities, you may lack the courage to tackle challenging projects. Security is a common aspiration, but setting and achieving goals might be hindered by a casual attitude.

- **Social Mobilization:** Extremely social, you possess a natural ability to mobilize large groups. While beautiful, there may be a lack of accuracy or math skills. Opening up to new experiences could be challenging, and focus might waver.

Lucky Attributes

• **Lucky Colors:** White and cream are your fortunate colors.

• **Lucky Gems:** Diamond, white sapphire, or quartz crystal bring luck.

• **Lucky Days:** Wednesday, Friday, and Saturday are favorable.

• **Lucky Numbers:** 6, 15, 24, 33, 42, 51, 60, 69, 78 are auspicious.

Famous Birthdays

Notable individuals born on February 6 include Christopher Marlowe, Kirpal Singh, Ronald Reagan, Zsa Zsa Gabor, Francois Truffaut, Mamie Van Doren, Mike Farrell, and Natalie Cole.

May your agreeable nature, Venusian charm, and artistic inclinations lead you to a life filled with harmonious relationships and creative fulfillment.

Astrological Profile for Those Born on February 7

If February 7 is your birthdate, your star sign is Aquarius, and your personal ruling planets are Uranus and Neptune. Let's explore the distinctive characteristics and influences shaping your unique personality.

Aquarian Traits

• **Unusual Ideas on Religion and Philosophy:** You possess original and unconventional ideas on religion and philosophy. Compassionate to sublime heights, you're willing to go to great lengths to help those in need. Balancing your needs is crucial to avoid becoming a victim of your altruistic endeavors.

• **Ruled by Uranus and Neptune:** The erratic Uranus and otherworldly Neptune govern your deepest nature. This combination signifies a craving for insight into cosmic consciousness, leading to sacrifices in your life.

• **Unconventional Path:** Following the inner promptings of your heart, you may turn a blind eye to external advice, preferring your own dictates. Sensitivity and self-sacrifice can, however, lead to a "victim" mentality. Careers in helping and healing professions bring fulfillment.

Social and Personal Attributes

• **Friendly and Eccentric:** Friendly and caring, you have a tendency to be eccentric. Current trends in your fields interest you, but negative tendencies can emerge. Managing your outgoing personality and isolated traits is essential.

• **Progressive Nature:** With a selfless and progressive nature, you dislike social inequalities and ignore diversity. Irony, jealousy, and impulsiveness may be part of your personality.

Romantic Inclinations

• **Keen Perception in Relationships:** In romance, your independent yet shy and confident nature shines. Keen perception and understanding make you a good judge of character and intentions. Be cautious of rejection, as your interest in relationships is deep. Accepting eccentricities enhances compatibility with Scorpios.

Lucky Attributes

• **Lucky Colors:** Darker green shades are fortunate for you.

• **Lucky Gems:** Turquoise, cat's eye, and chrysoberyl bring luck.

• **Lucky Days:** Saturdays and Mondays are favorable.

• **Lucky Numbers:** 7, 16, 25, 34, 43, 52, 61, 70, 79 are auspicious.

Famous Birthdays

Notable individuals born on February 7 include Sir Thomas More, Charles Dickens, Alfred Adler, Sinclair Lewis, Buster Crabbe, Wes Borland, Ashton Kutcher, and Tina Majorino.

May your unconventional spirit, compassionate nature, and keen perception lead you to a life filled with meaningful connections and personal fulfillment.

Astrological Profile for Those Born on February 8

If you were born on February 8, your star sign is Aquarius, and your personal ruling planets are Uranus and Saturn. Let's delve into the distinctive traits and influences that shape your character.

Aquarian Characteristics

• **Balancing Pessimism:** You may exhibit moments of pessimism, and it's crucial to balance your mind with joy, optimism, and inner sunshine. Reducing cynicism towards your life processes can lead to better results.

• **Financial Acumen:** Excelling with money, you display high resourcefulness and prudence in your dealings. Strong ambition and a solid sense of purpose contribute to your success.

• **Diametrically Opposed Energies:** Balancing the energies of Uranus and Saturn is key. Disciplined consistency and a sense of duty counterbalance the electrical impulses and quick thinking of Uranus. Cautious yet prudent, you navigate the delicate dance between imagination and conservatism.

• **Identifying with the Underdog:** Always identifying with the underdog and displaying fairness in work and play, you possess good executive ability and can manage others effectively.

Personality Traits

• **Visionary Thinker:** Quick-thinking and visionary, you excel in problem-solving and can see possibilities that others might overlook. Your creativity spans various fields, and your sense of humor is a valuable asset.

• **Drive to Succeed:** With an inborn drive to succeed, you project success and see the big picture. Your ability to enact brilliant ideas contributes to progress and reform, making you a potential leader in your chosen field.

Lucky Attributes

- **Lucky Colors:** Deep blue and black are fortunate for you.
- **Lucky Gem:** Blue sapphire is your lucky gem.
- **Lucky Days:** Wednesday, Friday, and Saturday are favorable.
- **Lucky Numbers:** 8, 17, 26, 35, 44, 53, 62, 71 are auspicious.

Famous Birthdays

Notable individuals born on February 8 include Robert Burton, John Ruskin, Jules Verne, Evangeline Adams, Martin Buber, Dame Edith Evans, Lana Turner, Jack Lemmon, James Dean, Nick Nolte, John Grisham, Seth Green, Alonzo Mourning, and Joshua Morrow.

May your balanced approach, financial acumen, and visionary thinking lead you to a life of success and fulfillment.

Astrological Profile for Those Born on February 9

If you were born on February 9, your star sign is Aquarius, and your personal ruling planets are Uranus and Mars. Let's explore the dynamic characteristics and influences that shape your unique personality.

Aquarian Traits

• **Bold and Energetic:** Governed by the bold and energetic Mars, you embody passion, activeness, and impulsive energy. Courageous, quick, and fiery, you thrive on taking on new projects and strive to be the first and best in your endeavors.

• **Precautionary Measures:** While your boldness is commendable, the combination of Uranus and Mars suggests a need for precaution. Prone to injury, it's essential to adhere to road rules, take precautions in health, and avoid a mad rush toward goals. Remember, "Slow and steady wins the race."

Personality Characteristics

• **Wisdom and Innocence:** Aquarians born on February 9 possess a unique combination of wisdom and innocence. Their willingness to act on ideas is evident in their work, overcoming life challenges with grace and persistence. They understand that success is a continual work in progress.

• **Aggressive Yet Gentle:** Known for their aggressiveness, individuals born on this day also have a gentle side. Rejection or criticism can deeply affect them, emphasizing the importance of staying calm under pressure. This day offers an opportunity to achieve lofty goals and be an inspiration.

Traits Suited for Success

• **Independence of Thought:** People born on February 9 are strong and capable of influencing those around them. Their independence of thought is a significant strength, but they should appreciate the contributions of others to avoid conflicts arising from arrogance.

Lucky Attributes

• **Lucky Colors:** Red, maroon, and scarlet are fortunate for you.

• **Lucky Gems:** Red coral and garnet are your lucky gems.

• **Lucky Days:** Monday, Tuesday, and Thursday are favorable.

• **Lucky Numbers:** 9, 18, 27, 36, 45, 54, 63, 72 are auspicious.

Famous Birthdays

Notable individuals born on February 9 include William H. Harrison, Dean Rusk, Mia Farrow, Ronald Colman, Joe Pesci, Danni Leigh, Charles Shaughnessy, and Amber Valletta.

May your boldness, passion, and wisdom guide you to success, and may you find balance in both your assertiveness and gentleness.

Astrological Profile for Those Born on February 10

If you were born on February 10, your star sign is Aquarius, and your personal ruling planets are Uranus and the Sun. Let's delve into the unique traits and influences that shape your personality.

Aquarian Attributes

- **Sun Amplification:** The Sun is prominent on your birthdate, endowing you with incredibly strong willpower and excellent health, accompanied by robust recuperative powers. This planetary alignment may spark a desire to express your creative ideas.

- **Generous Nature:** While you are a good helper, there might be instances where you feel that your efforts are not reciprocated adequately. It's essential to scrutinize your relationships, including peers, acquaintances, and even family members, as not everyone may respond to your generosity in the way you wish.

- **Lonely Paths:** At times, you may feel like you're treading a lonely path, but maintaining faith and heart will guide you through. The number 10, symbolized as the Wheel of Fortune, indicates that success is destined during the indicated years.

Love and Relationships

- **Romantic and Sincere:** Those born on February 10 are known for their romantic and sincere feelings. However, their trustful yet insecure nature might pose challenges in forming lasting relationships.

- **Compatible Matches:** Aquarians born on this date are attracted to Gemini or Libra, signs sharing their values and worldviews. They seek partners who understand their adventurous spirit. Taurus, Capricorn, and Scorpio are considered less compatible matches.

Lucky Attributes

- **Lucky Colors:** Yellow and gold are fortunate for you.
- **Lucky Gem:** Ruby is your lucky gem.

• **Lucky Days:** Sunday, Monday, and Thursday bring positive energy.

• **Lucky Numbers:** 1, 10, 19, 28, 37, 46, 55, 64, 73, and 82 hold significance for you.

Famous Birthdays

Notable individuals born on February 10 include Charles Lamb, Jimmy Durante, Robert Wagner, Robert Addie, Keri-Lynn, Laura Dern, and Sarah Aldrich.

May the amplified influence of the Sun bring you strength, creativity, and success, and may your generous nature find reciprocation in the meaningful connections you cultivate.

Astrological Profile for Those Born on February 11

If you were born on February 11, your star sign is Aquarius, and your personal ruling planets are Uranus and the Moon. Let's explore the unique traits and influences that shape your personality.

Aquarian Attributes

• **Excitable Energy:** You possess an abundance of excitable energy, leading to an overload on your nervous system. Being highly emotional, it's crucial to think carefully before reacting or entering relationships. Changeability in decisions is common, so standing firm after weighing pros and cons is advised.

• **Self-Examining Nature:** A commendable trait is your self-examining nature, allowing you to identify and rectify traits that need improvement.

• **Hidden Trials:** Be cautious of hidden trials and potential deception from others. Rushing into relationships, whether personal or business, without careful consideration may pose risks.

Personality and Relationships

• **Originality and Motivation:** You are an original and highly motivated individual who values others. However, a focus on your own needs may inadvertently neglect the well-being of others. Balancing self-interest with empathy is essential.

• **Healing Family Issues:** There's significant potential for you to address and heal family problems, leveraging your instinctive sense of empathy.

• **Compatibility:** In love, Aquarians born on February 11 are compatible with Aquarius, Libra, and Gemini due to similar personalities. A February 11-birthday horoscope can guide decisions in romantic relationships.

Lucky Attributes

• **Lucky Colors:** Cream and white bring positive energy into your life.

• **Lucky Gems:** Moonstone or pearl are your fortunate gems.

• **Lucky Days:** Monday, Thursday, and Sunday are favorable for you.

• **Lucky Numbers:** 2, 11, 20, 29, 38, 47, 56, 65, 74 hold significance for you.

Famous Birthdays

Notable individuals born on February 11 include Thomas A. Edison, Virginia E. Johnson, Leslie Nielsen, Tina Louise, Burt Reynolds, Sheryl Crow, Jennifer Aniston, and Jeffrey Meek.

May your excitable energy find balance, and may your self-examining nature guide you towards personal growth and fulfilling relationships.

Astrological Profile for Those Born on February 12

If you were born on February 12, your star sign is Aquarius, and your personal ruling planets are Uranus and Jupiter. Let's explore the beautiful energies that shape your personality.

Harmonious Energies

- **Uranus and Jupiter:** These ruling planets bring practical and intuitive energies into your life. The subharmonics of the Sun and Moon indicate a strong interest in the greater welfare of mankind. Your optimism shines, uplifting those around you, and your generosity is a true mark of your nature.

Personality Traits

- **Harmonious Relationships:** You have harmonious relationships with others, driven by your cautious yet reserved nature. Loyalty, care, and enthusiasm characterize your interactions. However, be mindful of being overly sensitive to criticism; overcoming this weakness will lead to more fulfilling relationships.

- **Eleventh House Influence:** The placement of the sun in your eleventh house enhances your desire for friendship, pursuing dreams, and achieving higher goals. Socializing, making new friends, and exploring the world enrich your life.

- **Aquarian Traits:** Independent, witty, and curious, Aquarians like you tend to hold onto relationships firmly. Loyalty is a defining trait, making breakups challenging. Dependability, honesty, and a broad-minded approach endear you to friends and family.

Numerology Insights

- **Root Number 3:** Your root number is 3, emphasizing "Innovation." Born on February 12, you may be prone to taking risks. While your unique approach is commendable, it's essential to balance innovation with caution to avoid unnecessary pitfalls.

Lucky Attributes

• **Lucky Colors:** Yellow is your fortunate color.

Cautionary Note

• **Risk-Taking Tendencies:** While your innovative spirit is an asset, be cautious not to be overly confident or impulsive in taking risks. Balancing boldness with thoughtful consideration ensures a more measured approach.

Embrace the positive energies of Uranus and Jupiter, continue spreading optimism, and let your innovative spirit thrive while navigating life's adventures with prudence.

Astrological Profile for Those Born on February 13

If you were born on February 13, your star sign is Aquarius, and your personal ruling planets are Uranus and Jupiter. Let's explore the energies surrounding your birth and how they shape your personality.

Key Energies

• **Uranus and Jupiter:** These ruling planets contribute to a powerful desire for material acquisition in your life. Success awaits you, especially if you maintain integrity and high ethical standards. While setbacks may occur, seek advice from experienced individuals, benefiting from their wisdom.

• **Number 13:** Considered a mysterious number associated with upheaval and transformation, understanding its vibration grants you great power and dominion over others. Embrace the transformative energies it brings.

Personality Traits

• **Charming and Serious:** As an Aquarian, you exude charm with a touch of seriousness. Careers that showcase your appealing personality are most beneficial. While appearing unstable, success is found in balancing personal and professional aspects. Focus on cultivating happiness in relationships and helping others for contentment.

• **Strong Willpower and Impulsiveness:** Born on February 13, you possess strong willpower and impulsiveness. Social and goal-oriented, Aquarians may face challenges in partnerships due to distractions and occasional poor decisions. Maintain balance by nurturing close relationships and ensuring civility with your partner.

Lucky Attributes

• **Lucky Colors:** Electric Blue, Electric White, and Multi-colors are auspicious for you.

• **Lucky Gems:** Hessonite garnet and agate bring luck and positive energies.

• **Lucky Days:** Sunday and Thursday are favorable days for you.

• **Lucky Numbers:** 4, 13, 22, 31, 40, 49, 58, 67, 76 are significant in your life.

Famous Birthdays

• Celebrate your birth alongside notable figures like Kim Novak, Peter Gabriel, Stockard Channing, and Richard Tyson.

Embrace the energies of Uranus and Jupiter, navigate the transformative power of the number 13, and let your charm and determination lead you to success, both personally and professionally.

Astrological Profile for Those Born on February 14

If you were born on February 14, your star sign is Aquarius, and your personal ruling planet is Uranus. Let's delve into the unique energies surrounding your birth and understand how they shape your personality.

Key Energies

- **Uranus Influence:** Your ruling planet, Uranus, imparts revolutionary energy, high sexuality, and potential trials. Prudence is essential to harness these potent energies effectively. Exercise self-control, especially in business speculation, as sudden changes may occur.

- **Love Life Dynamics:** Your love life may experience erratic patterns. Cultivate persistence and constancy for long-term satisfaction. Charm, perceptiveness, and humor characterize those born on February 14, enhancing their quick-witted and communicative traits.

Personality Traits

- **Charming and Perceptive:** February 14 individuals are often charming, perceptive, and humorous. Quick-witted with great communication skills, they possess an open mind and analytical thinking. Jobs requiring minimal energy, such as the silk industry, suit their preferences.

- **Relationship Challenges:** In relationships, they seek freedom but may find it challenging to share. Practicing meditation and maintaining a healthy lifestyle helps manage emotions. Born under the sign of Aquarius, they are passionate about love, often drawn to partners of the opposing astrological sign.

- **Optimistic and Wise:** Optimism and wisdom characterize those born on February 14. They take responsibility for their goals, integrating them into daily life. While pursuing personal objectives, they desire meaningful relationships, valuing thoughtfulness.

Lucky Attributes

• **Lucky Color:** Green is your auspicious color.

• **Lucky Gems:** Emerald, Aquamarine, or Jade bring luck and positive energies.

• **Lucky Days:** Wednesdays, Fridays, and Saturdays favor you.

• **Lucky Numbers:** 5, 14, 23, 32, 41, 50, 59, 68, 77 hold significance.

Famous Birthdays

• Celebrate alongside notable figures like Galileo, Jack Benny, James Hoffa, Hugh Downs, Magic Sam, Tim Buckley, Rob Thomas, Tarina Young, and Erin Torpey.

Embrace the revolutionary spirit of Uranus, navigate the dynamics of your love life with persistence, and let your charm and perceptiveness shine in both personal and professional spheres. May the lucky colors, gems, and numbers guide you toward a fulfilling journey.

Astrological Profile for Those Born on February 15

Born on February 15, you are an Aquarius with Venus and Uranus as your personal ruling planets, creating a glamorous and creative aura. Let's explore the unique energies and characteristics shaping your astrological profile.

Key Energies

• **Venus Influence:** Ruled by Venus, you possess creative abilities that may lead to a career in Fine Arts or Music. Your charm and dramatic nature enhance your speech, attracting and endearing others to you.

• **Magical Number 15:** The number 15, deemed mysterious and magical, bestows higher occult powers. Use these powers wisely, avoiding selfish motives. You'll notice their potential to achieve your goals.

Personality Traits

• **Unique and Intuitive:** February 15 individuals are unique, enjoying unconventional pursuits. Highly intuitive and friendly, they actively engage in social reform. Their sincerity and patience make them excellent trainers and teachers.

• **Romantic and Withdrawn:** While they tend to be romantic, they may become withdrawn and lonely if their partner is not in the same zodiac sign. Affinity for water is strong, making them receptive. Multiple partners might be a tendency, and they should be cautious about dependence on love relationships.

Lucky Attributes

• **Lucky Colors:** White and cream bring luck and harmony.

• **Lucky Gems:** Diamond, white sapphire, or quartz crystal enhance positive energies.

- **Lucky Days:** Wednesday, Friday, and Saturday favor your endeavors.
- **Lucky Numbers:** 6, 15, 24, 33, 42, 51, 60, 69, 78 hold significance.

Famous Birthdays

- Celebrate your birthday alongside notable figures like A.N. Whitehead, Caesar Romero, John Barrymore, Jane Seymour, Renee O'Connor, Jaromir Jagr, Galileo Galilea, and Elena Produnova.

Embrace the alluring energies of Venus, channel your creative talents, and use your occult powers responsibly. Your unique qualities make you an effective communicator and compassionate individual. May your journey be filled with artistic fulfillment and meaningful connections.

Astrological Profile for Those Born on February 16

Born on February 16, you are an Aquarius with Uranus and Neptune as your personal ruling planets, bestowing you with an incredible imagination and artistic inclinations. Let's explore the unique energies and characteristics shaping your astrological profile.

Key Energies

- **Imaginative Forces:** Ruled by Neptune and influenced by the Sun and Venus, your number 16 is associated with famous artists, musicians, and dancers. Your imagination is a powerful tool, offering creative potential.

- **Travel and Caution:** Travel, especially by water, is strongly indicated. However, caution is advised, particularly with fast cars, firearms, and sharp implements. Take care to avoid potential dangers associated with these elements.

- **Define Objectives:** While spiritual energies flow within you, ensure they are channeled toward defined objectives. Clearly define your goals and utilize your psychic and spiritual talents practically.

Personality Traits

- **Logical and Mindful:** Your horoscope indicates a person of great logicality, mindfulness, and dependability. Sensitivity and strong organizational skills define your character.

- **Charitable Inclinations:** Individuals born on February 16 often have a strong inclination to be involved in charitable causes or environmental activism, fighting for Mother Nature.

- **Creative Social Supporters:** Aquarians born on this day thrive in the company of creative social supporters who share their artistic passions and ideals.

Lucky Attributes

- **Lucky Colors:** Darker green shades bring luck and harmony.

- **Lucky Gems:** Turquoise, cat's eye, and chrysoberyl enhance positive energies.
- **Lucky Days:** Saturdays and Mondays favor your endeavors.
- **Lucky Numbers:** 7, 16, 25, 34, 43, 52, 61, 70, 79 hold significance.

Famous Birthdays

- Celebrate your birthday alongside notable figures like Sonny Bono, sharing the artistic and innovative energies associated with your birth date.

Embrace your imaginative forces, contribute to charitable causes, and surround yourself with supportive and creative individuals. As you navigate through life, remember to channel your spiritual energies toward practical objectives, defining clear goals for a fulfilling journey ahead.

Astrological Profile for Those Born on February 17

Born under the Aquarius sign with Uranus and Saturn as your personal ruling planets, your astrological profile unveils unique energies and characteristics that set the stage for a remarkable life.

Key Energies

• **Fortunate Vibration:** The vibration associated with the number 17 is highly prized by occultists, suggesting potential fame and a lasting legacy, either in this life or the next.

• **Executive Ability:** Endowed with executive ability, your heightened sensitivity allows you to perceive things others may overlook, providing a distinct advantage, especially in material realms.

• **Symbols of Peace and Love:** Your vibrations symbolize peace and love, empowering you with a revolutionary spirit, fortitude, and patience to conquer challenges head-on.

Personality Traits

• **Sensitivity:** Individuals born on February 17 tend to be sensitive, with a potential for eccentricity. Their open hearts and generous nature may make them prone to attracting fame.

• **Tech, Fashion, and Design:** Excelling in technology, fashion, and design, they display a natural desire to please others. However, they should guard against becoming too eccentric in their pursuits.

• **Privacy:** While quirky and hot-blooded, Aquarians value their privacy. Intrusive individuals may turn them off, and they are best matched with those who share similar values and respect their need for space.

Lucky Attributes

• **Lucky Colors:** Deep blue and black bring luck and harmony.

• **Lucky Gem:** Blue sapphire enhances positive energies.

• **Lucky Days:** Wednesdays, Fridays, and Saturdays favor your endeavors.

• **Lucky Numbers:** 8, 17, 26, 35, 44, 53, 62, 71 hold significance.

Famous Birthdays

• Celebrate your birthday alongside notable figures like Michael Jordan, Michael Bay, and Denise Richards, sharing the influential vibrations of the number 17.

Embrace your fortunate vibrations, leveraging your sensitivity and executive abilities to leave a lasting mark on the world. Whether it be in technology, fashion, or design, your open heart and generosity are likely to be remembered and celebrated.

Astrological Profile for Those Born on February 18

As an Aquarius born on February 18, your astrological profile reveals a unique blend of assertive energies, challenging emotions, and an unmatched fashion sense.

Key Energies

• **Aggressive Vibration:** Your aggressive vibration can be both an asset and a challenge. It may lead to dangerous ideas, and unchecked anger can be a downfall. However, this energy can be harnessed positively in litigation, arguments, and debates.

• **Talent for Healing:** Despite the challenges, you possess a talent for healing. The Martian vibration indicates that you follow your own path and are a trail-blazer, often finding your unique place in the world.

• **Genius or Insanity:** The number associated with your birth is linked to genius or insanity, leaving the choice in your hands. It's crucial to control emotions and channel higher energies.

Personality Traits

• **Impulsive and Emotional:** Born on February 18, you may be impulsive, impatient, and highly emotional. Accepting others' mistakes might be a challenge, but your leadership qualities make you a natural fit for roles that require people management.

• **Charming and Attractive:** Your romantic and attractive nature can be deceptive. While charming, you may display cattiness and overbearing tendencies. Your clear mind makes it difficult to deceive others.

Lucky Attributes

• **Lucky Colors:** Red, maroon, and scarlet bring luck and vibrancy.

• **Lucky Gems:** Red coral and garnet enhance positive energies.

• **Lucky Days:** Mondays, Tuesdays, and Thursdays favor your endeavors.

• **Lucky Numbers:** 9, 18, 27, 36, 45, 54, 63, 72 hold significance.
Famous Birthdays

• Join the ranks of notable individuals born on February 18, including John Travolta, Matt Dillon, and Molly Ringwald, who share the energetic vibrations of this distinctive date.

Embrace your assertive energies, use your talents for healing wisely, and navigate the fine line between genius and insanity. Your leadership qualities and unique fashion sense set you apart on this astrological journey.

Astrological Profile for Those Born on February 19

If you were born on February 19, your astrological profile as a Pisces reveals a combination of vitality, conflicting energies, and a tendency to be preoccupied with personal matters.

Key Energies

• **Vital Vibration:** Born on a day with vital vibrations, you possess great ability and physical strength. However, conflicting numbers and planetary influences create an inner conflict. Strive to balance self-focus with consideration for others.

• **Sheer Strength:** Your nature is marked by the ability to force through and push past obstacles using the sheer strength of your energy and vitality. While pushing forward is commendable, incorporating tact in your approach can enhance your effectiveness.

Personality Traits

• **Impressionable and Compassionate:** People born on February 19 are impressionable, compassionate, and spiritually inclined. Their emotions drive their actions, making them easily influenced. Sympathetic individuals make for good matches, while those lacking empathy should be avoided.

• **Restless Nature:** Restlessness may be a characteristic trait. While they have romantic instincts and are adventurous, their impulsive decisions might lead to unwise choices in relationships. Commitment can be challenging, and they may not tolerate clinginess.

Lucky Attributes

• **Lucky Colors:** Yellow and gold bring fortune and vibrancy.

• **Lucky Gem:** Ruby enhances positive energies.

• **Lucky Days:** Sunday, Monday, and Thursday favor your endeavors.

• **Lucky Numbers:** 1, 10, 19, 28, 37, 46, 55, 64, 73, and 82 hold significance.

Famous Birthdays

• Join the ranks of notable individuals born on February 19, including Copernicus, Smokey Robinson, and Amy Tan, who share the unique energy and conflicts associated with this date.

Embrace your vitality and strength, navigate the conflicts within, and strike a balance between personal focus and consideration for others. Your compassionate nature and romantic instincts make you a distinctive Piscean.

Astrological Profile for Those Born on February 20

If you were born on February 20, your astrological profile as a Pisces reveals ethereal vibrations and a harmonious connection between Neptune and the Moon.

Key Energies

- **Sweet and Ethereal:** Ruled by Neptune and the Moon, your vibrations are sweet, ethereal, and watery in nature. This combination bestows you with sweet speech, a fertile mind, and psychic vibrations, making you well-suited for New Age professions.

- **Community Minded:** You possess a strong sense of community and spontaneous ideas. While material success may face delays and hindrances, your feminine association allows you to navigate through obstacles, especially by connecting with females in the community.

Personality Traits

- **Responsibility and Commitment:** People born on February 20 are responsible and commit passionately to projects or ideas that align with their deepest desires. They thrive when dedicated to a cause that fulfills their sense of purpose.

- **Sensitivity:** Highly sensitive, you require a partner who understands and appreciates this aspect of your personality. Your passion and attention to detail can make you a bit challenging to love, but practicing patience and recognizing imperfections in both yourself and your partner is essential.

Lucky Attributes

- **Lucky Colors:** Cream and white bring luck and serenity.
- **Lucky Gems:** Moonstone or pearl enhance positive energies.
- **Lucky Days:** Monday, Thursday, and Sunday favor your endeavors.

- **Lucky Numbers:** 2, 11, 20, 29, 38, 47, 56, 65, 74 hold significance.

Famous Birthdays

- Join the ranks of notable individuals born on February 20, including Sidney Poitier, Cindy Crawford, and Kurt Cobain. Embrace your ethereal vibrations, community-minded spirit, and commitment to fulfilling endeavors.

Astrological Profile for Those Born on February 21st:

Pisces Unveiled: From Dreamy Depths to Radiant Heights

Your Pisces Essence:

• Ruling Planets: Neptune, the planet of dreams, illusions, and spirituality, combined with Jupiter, the planet of expansion, luck, and optimism, fuel your artistic soul and drive for knowledge.

• A Positive Incarnation: You've been blessed with vibrations of success and glory, hinting at a fulfilling journey where your artistic talents and wisdom shine.

• Universal Student: A thirst for knowledge and a deep capacity for learning define your path. Embrace your role as a lifelong student, soaking up wisdom from diverse sources.

Strengths and Gifts:

• Creative Brilliance: Your inherent Piscean sensitivity translates into stunning artistic expression. Explore music, writing, painting, or any medium that allows your soul to sing.

• Boundless Empathy: Your caring nature and strong desire to help others draw people to you. Embrace your role as a beacon of compassion and understanding.

• Intuitive Wisdom: Your connection to the unseen realm grants you profound insights. Trust your intuition and let it guide you through life's labyrinth.

• Resilient Spirit: Despite potential challenges, your optimism and Jupiter's blessings ensure you bounce back stronger after each hurdle.

Challenges and Growth Opportunities:

• Self-Perception vs. Reality: You may underestimate your own appeal. Remember, your inner beauty shines brightly, attracting genuine connections.

• Sensitivity and Criticism: Learn to differentiate constructive criticism from negativity. Embrace feedback as a chance to refine your work and grow.

• Environmental Influence: Choose your surroundings wisely. Immerse yourself in inspiring spaces that nurture your creativity and uplift your spirit.

• Emotional Boundaries: While empathy is a strength, setting healthy boundaries protects your emotional well-being. Learn to say "no" and prioritize your own needs.

Harnessing Your Potential:

• Creative Pursuits: Dive headfirst into artistic expression. Let your emotions flow onto canvas, into melodies, or through captivating words.

• Entrepreneurial Spirit: Your unique vision and Jupiter's touch of luck may guide you towards creating a successful business venture. Trust your instincts and pursue your ideas with passion.

• Spiritual Exploration: Delve into mindful practices, meditation, or the study of esoteric traditions. Deepen your connection to the cosmos and unlock your inner wisdom.

• Building Confidence: Affirm your inherent worth and celebrate your individuality. Remember, your sensitivity and artistic soul are your superpowers.

Lucky Colors: Embrace the sunshine! Yellow embodies your optimism, creativity, and joy. Surround yourself with this radiant hue to attract prosperity and illuminate your path.

Remember: Astrology offers a glimpse into your potential, but the tapestry of your life is woven by your choices and actions. Embrace your gifts, overcome your challenges, and paint your own masterpiece of existence.

Astrological Profile for Those Born on February 22

If you were born on February 22, your astrological profile as a Pisces reveals a unique combination of ruling planets—Neptune and Uranus—and the master vibration of triple 2.

Key Energies

- **Emotional Intensity:** The triple 2 vibration suggests an overemphasis on emotional energy. It's crucial for you to take control of these inner energies to prevent being overwhelmed by emotion.

- **Master Vibration:** As a person born on the 22nd, you possess a master vibration, indicating great potential. However, the key is to avoid laziness and work hard to capitalize on the opportunities presented to you.

Personality Traits

- **Creativity and Sensitivity:** Individuals born on February 22 exhibit an open, creative nature and are highly sensitive to criticism. This sensitivity, coupled with a compassionate and empathic disposition, makes them well-suited for roles involving problem-solving and variety.

- **Late Realization:** There may be a tendency to wait until the last moment to realize the significance of opportunities. It's essential to be proactive and put in the extra effort, avoiding regret for missed chances.

Relationships

- **Compassion and Empathy:** Regardless of sexual orientation or gender, those born on February 22 are compassionate, empathic partners. They lift others' spirits and seek relationships with shared values and visions for life.

- **Creative Passion:** Known for their creativity and passion in their work, they also possess a psychic ability to uplift others.

Lucky Attributes

• **Lucky Colors:** Electric Blue, Electric White, and Multi-colors bring positive vibes.

• **Lucky Gems:** Hessonite garnet and agate enhance luck.

• **Lucky Days:** Sunday and Thursday favor your endeavors.

• **Lucky Numbers:** 4, 13, 22, 31, 40, 49, 58, 67, 76 hold significance.

Famous Birthdays

• Join the ranks of notable individuals born on February 22, including George Washington, Frederic Chopin, Drew Barrymore, and the Crocodile Hunter, Steve Irwin.

Embrace your creative energy, empathic nature, and work ethic to fulfill your potential. So, dear Pisces of February 22nd, step into the light. Embrace your emotional depth, channel your artistic fire, and conquer the world with your gentle strength. Remember, the universe waits with bated breath to witness the masterpiece you were born to paint.

Astrological Profile for Those Born on February 23

Your Star Sign is Pisces

Your personal ruling planets are Neptune and Mercury.

The energy surrounding your birthdate is delightful, blending the dreamy influence of Neptune with the lively zest of Mercury. This creates a successful and dynamic vibration, infusing you with cleverness and a quick wit. Your ability to work well with calculations and business makes you popular among friends and earns respect in your chosen profession.

Career Path: With Mercury's influence over writing, languages, and journalism, these areas align seamlessly with your talents. Despite the many changes life may bring, the overall energy for the 23rd is fortunate and prosperous.

Love and Creativity: Craving love and embracing creativity, you find joy in nature and the company of talented individuals. However, narrow-mindedness and avarice are qualities that repel you. Your charming and intuitive nature makes you an excellent judge of character, but your versatility can lead to a reluctance to commit in relationships.

Saturn's Influence: Saturn, a patronizing planet, empowers you to tackle tasks and overcome obstacles. While possessing great listening skills, there's a risk of becoming manipulative when desires are unmet.

Personality Traits: Logical thinking, good communication, and an interest in the unusual and metaphysical characterize those born on February 23. Intelligent and generous, you express your feelings through art, but be mindful of your sensitivity, which can sometimes be overwhelming.

Lucky Charms:
- **Color:** Green

- **Gems:** Emerald, Aquamarine, or Jade
- **Days:** Wednesdays, Fridays, and Saturdays
- **Numbers:** 5, 14, 23, 32, 41, 50, 59, 68, 77

Famous People Born on Your Birthday: Samuel Pepys, William Shirer, Peter Fonda, Patricia Richardson, Ryan Cassidy, and Melinda Messenger.

Embrace the unique blend of Neptune's dreams and Mercury's intellect, dear Pisces of February 23, and navigate the prosperous journey that awaits you.

Astrological Profile for Those Born on February 24

Your Star Sign is Pisces

Pisces Zodiac Sign

Your personal ruling planets are Neptune and Venus.

Balancing Act: Your destiny unfolds as a struggle for balance, primarily between family and work. A highly strung nature often results from taking on more than you can handle. Emotional by essence, careful planning and avoiding overcommitment are crucial to prevent becoming a stranger within your own family due to overwork. The vibrations hint at a "workaholic" tendency.

Fortunate Connections: Despite the challenges, your destiny aligns you with influential people, particularly supportive women. The energy is promising for future success, especially in relationships with the opposite sex.

Nurturing and Generous: Born on February 24, you possess a nurturing temperament and Piscean intuition. Generosity and compassion define you, reflecting the selflessness characteristic of Pisces. Your creative spirit is complemented by a willingness to invent new ways to make things happen. Despite your giving nature, a touch of selfishness may surface, reminding you that receiving help is okay.

Lucky Charms:

- **Colors:** White and Cream
- **Gems:** Diamond, White Sapphire, or Quartz Crystal
- **Days:** Wednesday, Friday, and Saturday
- **Numbers:** 6, 15, 24, 33, 42, 51, 60, 69, 78

Famous People Born on Your Birthday: Wilhelm Grimm, Winslow Homer, Billy Zane, Edward James Olmos, and Manon Rheaume.

Navigate the delicate balance, embrace your nurturing spirit, and draw strength from the support of influential connections, dear Pisces born on February 24.

Astrological Profile for Those Born on February 25

Your Star Sign is Pisces

    Pisces Zodiac Sign

    Your personal ruling planet is Neptune.

Keen Observer: Born on February 25, you possess an innate ability to observe people. However, this may lead to moments of being overly critical. Trust issues may arise, and developing a sense of trust is key to finding the deeper meaning in relationships.

Power of Speech: Difficult periods may surface, often of your own making. Your speech holds significant power, impacting those around you. Trust becomes a central theme—trust others, and they will reciprocate.

Determined and Just: With a keen sense of justice, you're determined to support the right causes. Your ability to inspire others and positively influence your surroundings is notable. In matters of the heart, learning to be open and supportive is crucial, given past hurts.

Aspects and Reflections: Your birth date connects with various aspects of your life, including health and relationships. Patience is required in dealing with demanding relationships with siblings and neighbors. Finances may see improvement, but caution against slipping into old habits is advised.

Lucky Charms:

- **Colors:** Darker green shades
- **Gems:** Turquoise, Cat's Eye, Chrysoberyl
- **Days:** Saturdays and Mondays
- **Numbers:** 7, 16, 25, 34, 43, 52, 61, 70, 79

Famous People Born on Your Birthday: Pierre Renoir, John Foster Dulles, Meher-Bab, Jim Backhus, George Harrison, Tea Leoni, Julio Iglesias Jnr, Justin Jeffrey, and Justin Berfield.

Navigate trust, embrace your determination for justice, and let the power of your speech shape positive impacts, dear Pisces born on February 25.

Astrological Profile for Those Born on February 26

Your Star Sign is Pisces

    Pisces Zodiac Sign

    Your personal ruling planets are Neptune and Saturn.

    Saturn's Determined Path: Born on February 26, your personal ruling planets, Neptune and Saturn, indicate a path that may not always be considered lucky. Saturn's vibration suggests a challenging journey to achieve your goals, at times feeling alone and facing difficulties. Yet, your dedication and loyalty shine as your truly great personality traits.

    Wisdom Through Tough Times: Enduring tough experiences will transform into a wellspring of wisdom later in life. Despite challenges, your spiritual journey will develop, and Saturn's influence will bring you glory.

    Sensitivity and Attraction to Unusual: Your sense of the world makes you sensitive, drawing you towards unusual people. Curious and intuitive, you should not let your charming personality divert you from pursuing your career goals. Resist the temptation to accept work that doesn't align with your aspirations.

    Emotional and Resilient: Highly emotional, you dislike admitting defeat. Romantic and emotional tendencies are strong, but you require robust support to navigate life's challenges. Building a strong emotional connection is crucial for a fulfilling relationship. You are generous and attentive to loved ones, creating a flourishing love life when shared with someone adored.

    Lucky Charms:

- **Colors:** Deep blue and black
- **Gem:** Blue sapphire
- **Days:** Wednesday, Friday, and Saturday
- **Numbers:** 8, 17, 26, 35, 44, 53, 62, 71

Famous People Born on Your Birthday: Victor Hugo, Jackie Gleason, Fats Domino, Johnny Cash, Godfrey Cambridge, Michael Bolton, Mark Dacascos, and Alison Armitage.

Embrace the determined path, draw wisdom from challenges, and let your emotional resilience guide you, dear Pisces born on February 26.

Astrological Profile for Those Born on February 27

Your Star Sign is Pisces

    Pisces Zodiac Sign

    Your personal ruling planets are Neptune and Mars.

    Potential for Great Accomplishments: Born on February 27, your vibrations indicate great accomplishments in your future. Your soft inner emotional nature, combined with abundant energy, may lead to rushing and missed opportunities. Take a moment to pause, assess, and set your sights on roles in public office or government work.

    Creative, Just, and Sensitive: Possessing a creative mind, you approach dealings with justice and sensitivity. However, your highly independent nature may sometimes lead to overlooking the consequences of your actions. Consider the impact of your speech and actions to ensure harmony in your environment.

    Intense Emotions and Independence: People born on February 27 experience intense, deep emotions. While compassionate and empathic, independence and perseverance make them valuable assets. Discipline in relationships is essential, learning not to be overly demanding. Balancing emotional withdrawal with support for others is key.

    Supportive and Caring Pisces: Known for their supportive and caring nature, Pisces born on February 27 are driven and capable of overcoming challenges. They possess creativity to turn ideas into reality and assist others. Compassionate and kind, they excel in problem-solving. However, coping with anger or frustration may pose challenges.

    Lucky Charms:

- **Colors:** Red, maroon, and scarlet
- **Gems:** Red coral and garnet

- **Days:** Monday, Tuesday, and Thursday
- **Numbers:** 9, 18, 27, 36, 45, 54, 63, 72

Famous People Born on Your Birthday: H.W. Longfellow, Rudolph Steiner, John Steinbeck, Joan Bennett, Joanne Woodward, Elizabeth Taylor, Ralph Nader, and Adam Baldwin.

Embrace your potential for greatness, navigate intense emotions with grace, and let your caring nature shine, dear Pisces born on February 27.

Astrological Profile for Those Born on February 28

Your Star Sign is Pisces

    Pisces Zodiac Sign

    Your personal ruling planets are Neptune and Sun.

    Contradictory Energies: Born on February 28, your numbers and energies carry contradiction. While you work hard, returns may be limited, and challenges, including financial loss through legal matters, may arise. Guard against letting difficult periods color your perception entirely. A melancholic energy surrounds you, and you tend to see the downside of things at times.

    Dreamy and Generous: Individuals born on February 28, the second day in the lunar calendar, are often dreamy and generous. With a youthful outlook, they make great teachers and inspirational leaders. However, beware of the potential downsides associated with this birthdate.

    Ambitious and Demanding: Ambitious and sometimes demanding, those born on February 28 can be impulsive, potentially upsetting partners. Clear goals bring dedication and hard work, but fragility in health and proneness to injury should be considered.

    Exceptional Emotional Understanding: People born on this day have an exceptional emotional understanding of others, easily connecting with a broad range of people. Their outgoing personality may lead them into the spotlight, but challenges in focusing on relationships and indecision may arise.

    Utilizing Weaknesses for Growth: While dealing with weaknesses, individuals born on February 28 should strive to utilize them for personal growth and avoid repeating mistakes. They are urged to embrace their unique qualities and navigate challenges with resilience.

Lucky Charms:
- **Colors:** Yellow and gold
- **Gem:** Ruby
- **Days:** Sunday, Monday, and Thursday
- **Numbers:** 1, 10, 19, 28, 37, 46, 55, 64, 73, 82

Famous People Born on Your Birthday: Montaigne, Zero Mostel, Stephanie Beacham, Bernadette Peters, John Turturro, Peter Britt, and Eric Lindros.

Embrace the contradictions, channel your dreamy nature into inspiration, and use challenges as stepping stones, dear Pisces born on February 28.

Astrological Profile for Those Born on February 29

Your Star Sign is Pisces

  Pisces Zodiac Sign

  Your personal ruling planets are Neptune and Moon.

  Natural Flair for Social Connections: Born on February 29, you excel in social spheres, making careers in travel, sales, or the hospitality industry particularly well-suited for you. Your natural flair for relating to people is evident, and you possess a hot-natured, impulsive energy that drives you to get ahead.

  Curb Urgency and Measure Generosity: While your enthusiasm and generosity are admirable, be cautious not to give too much away, especially to potentially unreliable friends seeking advantage. Your childlike sense of enthusiasm and keen sense of humor make you well-suited for roles like a romantic poet or a leader. However, it's crucial to balance enthusiasm with discernment.

  Continuous Learning and Analytical Development: People born on February 29 thrive on continuous learning and possess strong analytical abilities. Strive to overcome indecision and moodiness, acknowledging the need for personal growth. Embrace change and avoid letting habits dictate your life.

  Cherishing Independence in Relationships: In the realm of relationships, those born on this date may face challenges in deciding whether they prefer solitude or companionship. Cultivate independence, maintaining a life separate from relationships. Trust is essential, and being with someone trustworthy allows you to enjoy companionship without dominating your life.

  Lucky Charms:

  - **Colors:** Cream and white
  - **Gems:** Moonstone or pearl

- **Days:** Monday, Thursday, and Sunday
- **Numbers:** 2, 11, 20, 29, 38, 47, 56, 65, 74

Famous People Born on Your Birthday: G. Rossini.

Navigate your unique path with the wisdom gained from continuous learning, and let your natural flair for social connections shine, dear Pisces born on February 29.

Insights into Aquarius and Pisces Compatibility

Let's delve deeper into the characteristics and compatibility of individuals born under Aquarius and Pisces.

Aquarius (January 20 - February 18):

Personality Traits:

1. **Innovative Thinkers:** Aquarians are known for their innovative and forward-thinking minds. They enjoy exploring new ideas and concepts.
2. **Independent Spirits:** Independence is a key trait; they value their freedom and often seek unconventional paths.
3. **Humanitarian Focus:** Aquarians have a strong sense of social justice and often engage in activities that contribute to the greater good.

Compatibility:

1. **Gemini (May 21 - June 20):** Both air signs, Gemini and Aquarius, share a love for intellectual pursuits and engaging conversations.
2. **Libra (September 23 - October 22):** Libra's diplomatic nature complements Aquarius, and together they can create harmonious relationships.
3. **Sagittarius (November 22 - December 21):** Both signs appreciate adventure and exploration, making them compatible in their quest for new experiences.

Areas of Growth:

1. **Emotional Expression:** Aquarians may need to work on

expressing their emotions more openly to deepen their connections.

2. **Patience:** As visionaries, Aquarians may benefit from cultivating patience, especially in collaborative endeavors.

Pisces (February 19 - March 20):

Personality Traits:

1. **Empathetic Souls:** Pisceans are highly empathetic and often absorb the emotions of those around them.
2. **Creative Imaginations:** They possess vivid imaginations and are drawn to artistic pursuits, expressing themselves through various forms of creativity.
3. **Intuitive Nature:** Pisceans have a strong intuitive sense, making them attuned to the emotions and needs of others.

Compatibility:

1. **Cancer (June 21 - July 22):** Both water signs, Cancer and Pisces, share deep emotional connections and a nurturing approach to relationships.
2. **Scorpio (October 23 - November 21):** Scorpio's intensity aligns well with Pisces' emotional depth, creating a powerful connection.
3. **Capricorn (December 22 - January 19):** Capricorn's practicality can complement Pisces' dreamy nature, creating a balanced partnership.

Areas of Growth:

1. **Boundaries:** Pisceans may need to establish healthy boundaries to avoid becoming overwhelmed by others' emotions.

2. **Decision-Making:** Pisceans might benefit from developing decision-making skills to navigate life's challenges with more confidence.

Compatibility Notes:

• **Aquarius and Pisces:** While both signs can appreciate each other's uniqueness, there may be challenges due to their differing approaches to life. Aquarius' rationality may clash with Pisces' emotional depth, but with open communication, they can find a balance.

Individual compatibility is complex and depends on the complete birth chart. It's always valuable to consider other factors like moon signs, rising signs, and planetary placements for a more nuanced understanding of relationships.

Book Overview: "The Secret Language of Birthdays"

Book Teachings

"The Secret Language of Birthdays" delves into the fusion of astrology, numerology, and psychic intuition to provide a comprehensive guide to understanding personalities. Here's what the book teaches:

1. **Astrological Insights:** Explores the significance of each birthday, offering detailed astrological profiles for each day of the year.

2. **Numerological Integration:** Integrates numerology to enhance the depth of insights, examining life path numbers, expression numbers, and soul urge numbers.

3. **Personalized Profiles:** Provides personalized profiles for individuals based on their birth date, encompassing characteristics, tendencies, and potential life paths.

4. **Astrological Elements:** Delves into the elements (fire, earth, air, water) and modalities (cardinal, fixed, mutable) to further enrich the understanding of individual traits.

5. **Planetary Influences:** Examines how each planet influences personality traits, behaviors, and life events, offering a nuanced perspective on astrological makeup.

6. **Compatibility and Relationships:** Guides readers in understanding astrological factors influencing interpersonal relationships, fostering better communication and connection.

7. **Astrological Transits:** Explores the impact of planetary transits on various life events, providing insights into timing, challenges, and opportunities.

8. **Numerology Integration:** Incorporates numerology for a

comprehensive understanding, analyzing life path numbers, expression numbers, and personality numbers.

9. **Practical Applications:** Offers practical guidance on applying astrological insights in daily life, including decision-making, time management, and relationship enhancement.

10. **Case Studies:** Illustrates real-life examples demonstrating how astrological influences impact individuals in areas such as career, relationships, and personal development.

Benefits

1. **Self-Discovery:** Readers gain a profound understanding of their own personalities, strengths, and potential life paths.
2. **Enhanced Relationships:** Insights into astrological compatibility and relationship dynamics contribute to healthier and more fulfilling connections.
3. **Informed Decision-Making:** Practical applications empower individuals to make decisions aligned with favorable astrological influences.
4. **Timing and Planning:** Understanding planetary transits aids in timing significant life events, fostering optimal outcomes.
5. **Holistic Well-Being:** Integration of astrology and numerology supports a holistic approach to well-being, encompassing physical, emotional, and spiritual aspects.
6. **Personal Growth:** The teachings encourage continuous self-reflection and personal growth, fostering a lifelong journey of understanding and empowerment.

In summary, "The Secret Language of Birthdays" serves as a comprehensive guide to unlocking the mysteries of personality and life events through the lens of astrology and numerology, providing practical tools for self-discovery and personal development.

How to Read a Birth Chart: Astrology for Beginners?

If life feels like a puzzle, your birth chart might hold the missing pieces. Understanding how to read your birth chart unveils insights into your personality, desires, behaviors, and motivations. The celestial ballet of stars and planets at the moment you were born shapes your cosmic fingerprint. Let's embark on a beginner-friendly guide to decoding the cosmic language and discovering your astrological destiny.

Deciphering Your Birth Chart

Your birth chart is a celestial snapshot, capturing the positions of stars and planets at your birth. While it's a guiding map, remember, it doesn't control your destiny—it's a tool for self-discovery.

1. Moon Signs and Sun Signs

- **Identify Your Essence:** Start with your sun and moon signs, representing the positions of the sun and moon at your birth. These cosmic influencers paint the canvas of your personality and emotional landscape.

2. Your Zodiac Sign

- **The Ascendant Sign:** Uncover your ascendant sign or rising sign, rising above the eastern horizon at your birth. It's your planetary chart ruler, adding nuances to your cosmic identity.

3. Impact of Planet Alignment

- **Celestial Playmakers:** Dive into the impact of all celestial bodies—sun, moon, and planets. Each planet brings unique traits, talents, and passions. Learn how they choreograph the cosmic dance of your life.

  - **Inner vs. Outer Planets:** Understand the dynamic interplay between inner planets (Mercury, Venus, Mars) offering daily bursts of energy, and outer planets (Jupiter,

Saturn, Uranus, Neptune, Pluto) influencing major life events more gradually.

4. Understanding Birth Chart Houses

• **Cosmic Real Estate:** Your birth chart is divided into twelve houses, each governing a life aspect.

> • *Example: House Seven - Marriage:* Ruled by Libra, it oversees relationships, intimacy, and partnerships.

Reading Your Birth Chart: A Beginner's Adventure

If you're a novice, fear not. Reading your birth chart is an exciting journey, not a daunting task. Focus on your rising zodiac sign, corresponding house, and planetary alignment. This trio unveils the cosmic story of your life, making astrology an accessible guide to self-discovery.

Embrace Your Astrological Blueprint

Your birth chart is a personalized cosmic manual. By embracing its wisdom, you tap into the energy of the stars. The valuable insights into your desires become a compass for success. Once you've unlocked the secrets of your birth chart, your cosmic journey begins, empowered by the wisdom of the cosmos.

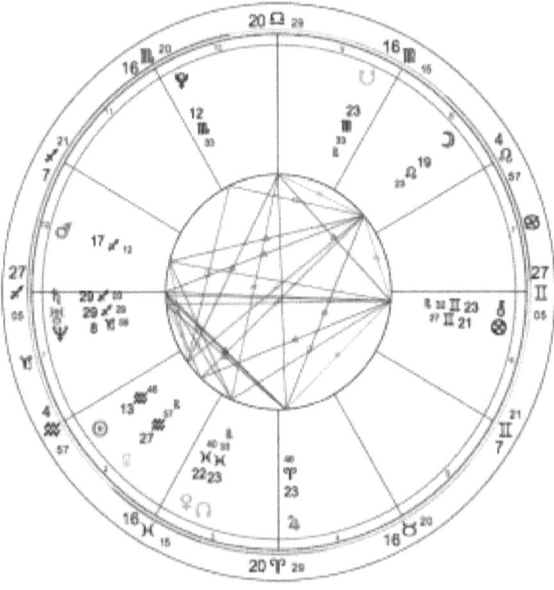

Brief Overview of Astrology and Its Significance

Astrology is an ancient belief system that examines the positions and movements of celestial bodies to gain insights into human affairs and natural events. It operates on the principle that the positions of planets, the sun, and the moon at the time of one's birth can influence their personality, behavior, and life path.

Key Components:

1. **Zodiac Signs:** Astrology is organized around the twelve zodiac signs, each associated with specific dates. These signs represent different personality traits and characteristics.
2. **Planetary Influences:** The planets, including Mercury, Venus, Mars, Jupiter, Saturn, and others, play a crucial role. Their positions in the birth chart can indicate specific influences on an individual's traits.
3. **Houses:** Astrological houses represent different aspects of life, such as relationships, career, and home. The placement of planets in these houses adds layers to the interpretation.

Significance in Understanding Personalities:

1. **Self-Discovery:** Astrology offers a tool for self-discovery, encouraging individuals to explore their strengths, weaknesses, and unique qualities.
2. **Behavioral Patterns:** By analyzing the birth chart, astrologers can identify behavioral patterns, helping individuals understand why they may react to certain situations in specific ways.
3. **Life Path Guidance:** Astrology provides insights into potential life paths, guiding individuals to align their choices with cosmic energies for personal growth.

In essence, astrology serves as a symbolic language that, when decoded, provides a framework for understanding and navigating the complexities of human personalities.

Basic Astrological Concepts

1. Zodiac Signs:
- The zodiac is divided into twelve signs, each associated with specific dates. These signs, such as Aries, Taurus, and Gemini, represent different personality traits and characteristics.
- Individuals are classified under a particular zodiac sign based on their birthdate, indicating the sun's position at that time.

2. Planets:
- Planets in astrology symbolize different facets of life and influence personality traits. Common planets include Mercury (communication), Venus (love and beauty), and Mars (energy and drive).
- The position of planets in the birth chart reveals their influence on an individual's behavior and life path.

3. Houses:
- Astrological houses are twelve divisions that represent specific areas of life. Each house corresponds to a different aspect, such as relationships, career, or home.
- The planets' placement in these houses provides insights into how various life areas are influenced.

Understanding Interplay:
- The combination of zodiac signs, planets, and houses in a birth chart creates a unique cosmic blueprint for an individual.
- For instance, a person with the sun in Leo (zodiac sign), Venus in Libra (planet), and these planets in the seventh house (house) may exhibit strong leadership qualities in relationships.

Key Terms:
- **Ascendant (Rising Sign):** The zodiac sign rising on the eastern horizon at the time of birth, influencing how a person presents themselves.

• **Moon Sign:** Reflects emotions and inner self, adding depth to the sun sign's description.

In summary, grasping these fundamental concepts lays the groundwork for interpreting a birth chart and understanding the intricate interplay of astrological elements.

Birth Chart Interpretation

Constructing a Birth Chart:
   1. Gather Birth Information:

- Collect precise details: date, time, and place of birth.
- The accuracy of the birth chart relies on this information.

2. Identify Natal Planets and Signs:

- Utilize an astrological software or consult an astrologer to identify the position of each planet in specific zodiac signs.

3. Determine Houses:

- Map the planets to the corresponding astrological houses based on the birth chart.

4. Ascendant and Descendant:

- Identify the ascendant (rising sign) and descendant to understand the individual's outward demeanor and interpersonal dynamics.

Interpreting the Birth Chart:
1. Sun Sign Interpretation:

- Explore the characteristics associated with the sun sign. It reflects the core identity and conscious self.

2. Moon Sign Insights:

- Examine the moon sign for emotional tendencies and responses, providing depth to the sun sign's traits.

3. Ascendant Influence:

• The rising sign influences how others perceive an individual. Consider its traits in the context of the person's overall chart.

4. Planetary Aspects:

• Investigate aspects (angular relationships) between planets. For example, a harmonious aspect between Venus and Mars may indicate a balanced approach to love and desire.

5. House Significance:

• Analyze the planets' placement in houses to understand specific life areas impacted, such as career, relationships, or spirituality.

6. Dominant Elements and Modalities:

• Identify the dominant elements (fire, earth, air, water) and modalities (cardinal, fixed, mutable) in the chart, offering additional insights into personality.

7. Transits and Progressions:

• Consider current planetary transits and progressions for a dynamic interpretation of life events and potential changes.

Guidelines:
• Encourage individuals to embrace the strengths and challenges indicated by their chart.

• Highlight the fluidity of astrological influences, emphasizing free will and personal growth.

In essence, the birth chart serves as a celestial map, guiding individuals toward self-discovery and a deeper understanding of their unique cosmic blueprint.

Lunar Guidance: Moon's Secrets in Your Birth Chart

The Moon is considered one of the most important celestial bodies in astrology, and its placement in your birth chart has significant meaning. Here's how the Moon relates to your birthchart:

1. **Inner World:** The Moon is a celestial storyteller, narrating the intricate tale of your inner world. In your birth chart, it functions as a cosmic compass, pointing towards your emotional landscape and subconscious desires. Here's what the Moon unveils:

The Moon represents your emotions, intuition, subconscious mind, and needs for security and comfort. Its position in your birth chart reveals how you process and express emotions, your emotional needs, and how you seek comfort and nurturing.

- **Emotional Processing:** Explore how you process emotions, whether through introspection or outward expression.

- **Intuition and Insights:** Understand the role of intuition in decision-making and how the Moon shapes your gut instincts.

- **Needs for Security:** Delve into your fundamental needs for security, comfort, and emotional well-being.

2. **Sign and House:** The Moon, adorned with the zodiac's hues, paints a unique emotional portrait. Its position in a particular sign and house crafts a masterpiece of your emotional tendencies. Let's explore further:

The Moon's sign in your birth chart indicates your fundamental emotional tendencies and how you react to different situations. Each sign has its own emotional expression, from the nurturing Cancer to the independent Aquarius.

The house where the Moon falls in your birth chart reveals the area of life where emotions play a significant role. For example, a Moon in the 4th house might indicate strong attachments to family or a focus on creating a secure home environment.

- **Zodiac Emotional Flavors:** Each zodiac sign colors your emotional responses differently. Dive into the nuances, from the nurturing tendencies of Cancer to the independent spirit of Aquarius.

- **House Significance:** Uncover how the Moon's placement in a specific house influences your emotional connection to that area of life. For example, a Moon in the 4th house may signify a profound emotional tie to family and home.

3. **Aspects:** The Moon dances with other celestial partners in your birth chart, creating a celestial symphony of emotional experiences. Explore the different notes:

The Moon's aspects to other planets in your birth chart show how your emotions interact with other areas of your life. Positive aspects might indicate emotional stability and ease of expression, while challenging aspects could point to emotional blocks or difficulties.

- **Positive Aspects:** Discover how harmonious connections enhance emotional stability and ease of expression.

- **Challenging Aspects:** Navigate emotional challenges indicated by aspects, offering insights into areas of growth and self-awareness.

4. **Moon Phases:** The Moon's phase at your birth adds a poetic layer to your personality. Let's delve into the lunar phases:

The phase of the Moon at your birth can also offer insights into your personality. A Full Moon baby might be more expressive and outward-focused, while a New Moon baby might be more introspective and private.

- **Full Moon Energy:** Experience the expressive and outward-focused nature associated with a Full Moon birth.

- **New Moon Essence:** Embrace the introspective and private qualities linked to a New Moon birth.

5. **Beyond Basics:** To truly understand the Moon's influence, consider the following celestial nuances:

Exploring the Moon's position in your birth chart goes beyond just the sign and house. You can also analyze its dignity (strength or weakness), declinations (how far it is from the equator), and other astrological concepts for a deeper understanding.

- **Dignity of the Moon:** Explore the strength or weakness of the Moon in your chart, providing insights into its potency.

- **Declinations:** Understand how the Moon's distance from the equator adds a unique dimension to its influence.

Astrology is a complex and nuanced system, and interpreting the Moon's placement in your birth chart requires considering all these factors and more. It's always best to consult a qualified astrologer for a personalized reading.

If you'd like to delve deeper, I can tell you more about specific aspects of the Moon in your birth chart or answer any questions you have about interpreting its placement. Just provide me with your birth date and time, and I'll be happy to assist you further.

I hope this gives you a good starting point for understanding the Moon's relationship with your birth chart!

Remember, the richness of astrology unfolds in layers. For a personalized reading, consult a qualified astrologer who can navigate the cosmic tapestry of your birth chart.

If you're eager to explore specific facets, share your birth date and time for a deeper dive into the Moon's profound connection with your celestial self. I'm here to guide you on this cosmic journey, adding splendor to your understanding of the Moon's dance in your birth

2024 Moon Phase Calendar

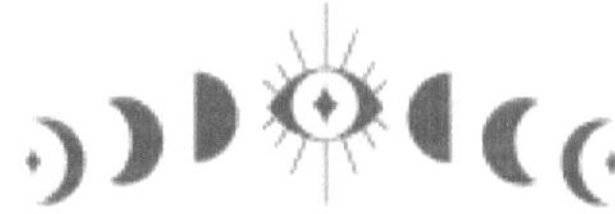

chart!

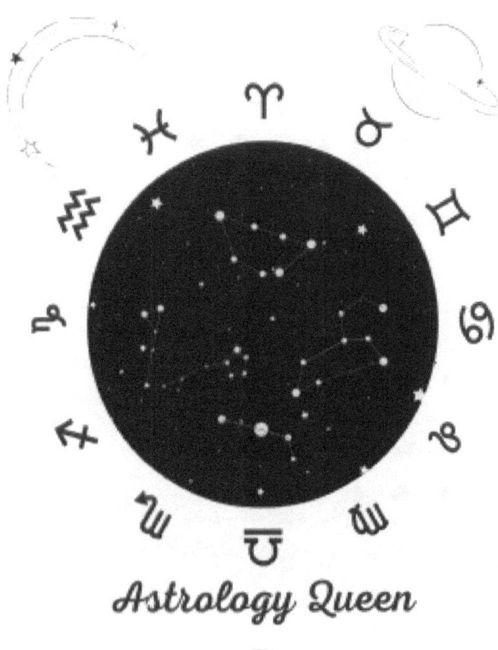

Astrology Queen

2024 Astrological Dates

Directs

Jan 2	Mercury	Sagittarius
Jan 27	Uranus	Taurus
Apr 25	Mercury	Aries
Aug 24	Mercury	Leo
Oct 12	Pluto	Capricorn
Nov 15	Saturn	Pisces
Dec 7	Neptune	Pisces
Dec 15	Mercury	Sagittarius
Dec 29	Chiron	Aries

Retrogrades

Apr 1	Mercury	Aries
May 2	Pluto	Aquarius
Jun 29	Saturn	Pisces
Jul 2	Neptune	Pisces
Jul 26	Chiron	Aries
Aug 5	Mercury	Virgo
Sep 1	Uranus	Taurus
Oct 9	Jupiter	Gemini
Nov 26	Mercury	Sagittarius
Dec 6	Mars	Leo

Meteor Showers

Quadrantids	04-Jan-2024
Alpha Centaurids	09-Feb-2024
Eta Virginias	14-Mar-2024
Kappa Serpentis	09-Apr-2024
Lyrids	22-Apr-2024
Pi Puppis	23-Apr-2024
Eta Aquariids	09-May-2024
Eta Lyrids	09-May-2024
Botiids	27-Jun-2024
South. Delta Aquariids	30-Jul-2024
Alpha Capricornids	30-Jul-2024
South. Delta Aquariids	04-Aug-2024
Perseids	12-Aug-2024
Kappa Cygnus	18-Aug-2024
Alpha Aurigids	31-Aug-2024
Capricorn ds	02-Oct-2024
Camelopardalis	05-Oct-2024
Draconis	08-Oct-2024
Orionids	21-Oct-2024
Northern Taurids	06-Nov-2024
Southern Taurids	17-Nov-2024
Leonidas	06-Nov-2024
Geminids	21-Nov-2024
Alpha Monocerotids	15-Dec-2024
Ursids	22-Dec-2024
Comae Berenicids	25-Dec-2024

Finding the Right Astrology Software

for Birth Chart Readings

If you're looking for reliable astrology software to generate accurate birth chart readings, here are some top choices:

1. Astrolabe's Solar Fire Gold[1]: A comprehensive software program known for its features.
2. Jagannatha Hora[2]: Highly recommended and available for free, offering quick and easy birth chart readings.
3. Sirius[3]: Considered one of the most robust astrology software, perfect for in-depth chart research.
4. AstroWOW[4]: User-friendly software that provides a guide to interpreting astrological insights.
5. TimePassages[5]: Ideal for both beginners and professionals, offering astrological insights used by experts.
6. Best Astrology Software in 2023[6]: Various options like Parashara's Light, LeoStar Professional, Red Astro Premium 8.0, and more.

When exploring these options, consider your skill level, preferences, and the specific features each software offers. Whether you're a beginner or an experienced astrologer, these tools provide the necessary resources for insightful birth chart readings.

---

1. https://coolwisdombooks.com/astrology-software/

2. https://www.quora.com/Which-is-the-best-astrology-app-website-for-birth-chart-reading

3. https://www.astrologyuniversity.com/astrology-software/

4. https://www.astrowow.com/astrology-software

5. https://www.astrograph.com/astrology-software/

6. https://www.techjockey.com/category/astrology-software

Zodiac Signs and Characteristics

1. Aries (March 21 - April 19):
- *Traits:* Energetic, assertive, and adventurous.
- *Tendencies:* Natural leaders, inclined to take initiative, and thrive on challenges.

2. Taurus (April 20 - May 20):
- *Traits:* Patient, reliable, and grounded.
- *Tendencies:* Appreciates stability, enjoys sensory pleasures, and values loyalty.

3. Gemini (May 21 - June 20):
- *Traits:* Curious, adaptable, and communicative.
- *Tendencies:* Social butterflies, versatile thinkers, and love intellectual stimulation.

4. Cancer (June 21 - July 22):
- *Traits:* Nurturing, empathetic, and intuitive.
- *Tendencies:* Family-oriented, protective, and attuned to emotional dynamics.

5. Leo (July 23 - August 22):
- *Traits:* Charismatic, confident, and passionate.
- *Tendencies:* Natural performers, seek attention, and value generosity.

6. Virgo (August 23 - September 22):
- *Traits:* Detail-oriented, analytical, and practical.
- *Tendencies:* Perfectionists, service-oriented, and possess a strong work ethic.

7. Libra (September 23 - October 22):
- *Traits:* Diplomatic, charming, and cooperative.
- *Tendencies:* Value harmony, seek balance, and enjoy social connections.

8. Scorpio (October 23 - November 21):

- *Traits:* Intense, determined, and mysterious.
- *Tendencies:* Seek depth in relationships, resilient, and possess strong intuition.

9. Sagittarius (November 22 - December 21):

- *Traits:* Optimistic, adventurous, and philosophical.
- *Tendencies:* Love exploration, freedom, and have a jovial spirit.

10. Capricorn (December 22 - January 19): - *Traits:* Ambitious, disciplined, and responsible. - *Tendencies:* Goal-oriented, value tradition, and exhibit strong leadership.

11. Aquarius (January 20 - February 18): - *Traits:* Innovative, independent, and humanitarian. - *Tendencies:* Embrace uniqueness, forward-thinking, and value social causes.

12. Pisces (February 19 - March 20): - *Traits:* Compassionate, artistic, and intuitive. - *Tendencies:* Dreamy, sensitive, and often blur boundaries between reality and fantasy.

Understanding the distinct characteristics of each zodiac sign provides valuable insights into individual traits and behaviors, fostering better self-awareness and interpersonal understanding.

Planetary Influences on Personality

1. Sun (☉):
- *Influence:* Represents the core identity and conscious self.
- *Effects:* Shapes individuality, ego, and vitality. Affects leadership qualities and life purpose.

2. Moon (☽):
- *Influence:* Reflects emotions and inner self.
- *Effects:* Governs emotional responses, instincts, and nurturing tendencies. Influences mood and reactions.

3. Mercury (☿):
- *Influence:* Governs communication and intellect.
- *Effects:* Shapes thinking processes, learning style, and communication methods. Impacts how one processes information.

4. Venus (♀):
- *Influence:* Rules love, beauty, and aesthetics.
- *Effects:* Affects romantic inclinations, artistic expressions, and social interactions. Influences preferences in relationships.

5. Mars (♂):
- *Influence:* Symbolizes energy, drive, and assertiveness.
- *Effects:* Shapes ambition, competitiveness, and the approach to challenges. Governs physical energy and sexuality.

6. Jupiter (♃):
- *Influence:* Represents expansion, abundance, and growth.
- *Effects:* Influences optimism, abundance, and the pursuit of knowledge. Governs luck and opportunities.

7. Saturn (♄):
- *Influence:* Governs discipline, responsibility, and structure.
- *Effects:* Shapes perseverance, sense of duty, and ambition. Governs lessons and challenges for personal growth.

8. Uranus (♅):

- *Influence:* Symbolizes innovation, originality, and unpredictability.

- *Effects:* Affects the desire for freedom, unconventional thinking, and sudden changes. Governs breakthroughs.

9. Neptune (♆):

- *Influence:* Rules imagination, dreams, and spirituality.

- *Effects:* Shapes creativity, intuition, and the inclination towards spiritual pursuits. Influences the perception of reality.

10. Pluto (♇): - *Influence:* Symbolizes transformation, regeneration, and power. - *Effects:* Governs deep transformation, intensity, and the ability to overcome challenges. Influences profound changes.

Understanding how each planet influences personality traits provides a nuanced perspective on an individual's astrological makeup. The interplay of these celestial forces contributes to the complexity and uniqueness of each person's character.

Astrological Elements and Modalities

Astrological Elements:

1. Fire (Aries, Leo, Sagittarius):

- *Characteristics:* Energetic, passionate, and spontaneous.

- *Influence:* Individuals with fire signs are often driven by enthusiasm, creativity, and a desire for adventure.

2. Earth (Taurus, Virgo, Capricorn):

- *Characteristics:* Practical, grounded, and dependable.

- *Influence:* Earth signs emphasize stability, reliability, and a connection to the physical world.

3. Air (Gemini, Libra, Aquarius):

- *Characteristics:* Intellectually curious, communicative, and social.

- *Influence:* Air signs prioritize mental stimulation, communication, and social interactions.

4. Water (Cancer, Scorpio, Pisces):

- *Characteristics:* Emotional, intuitive, and empathetic.

- *Influence:* Water signs are often attuned to emotions, intuition, and have a deep connection to the emotional world.

Astrological Modalities:

1. **Cardinal Signs (Aries, Cancer, Libra, Capricorn):**

• *Characteristics:* Initiators, leaders, and proactive.

• *Influence:* Cardinal signs are known for starting new ventures, taking charge, and initiating change.

2. **Fixed Signs (Taurus, Leo, Scorpio, Aquarius):**

• *Characteristics:* Stable, determined, and resistant to change.

• *Influence:* Fixed signs embody persistence, determination, and stability in the face of challenges.

3. **Mutable Signs (Gemini, Virgo, Sagittarius, Pisces):**

• *Characteristics:* Adaptable, flexible, and open to change.

• *Influence:* Mutable signs are versatile, open-minded, and comfortable navigating transitions.

Relation to Birthdays:
• **Birthday Element:** The element of the birthday sign contributes to an individual's fundamental nature. For example, a fire sign birthday suggests a dynamic and energetic personality.
• **Birthday Modality:** The modality of the birthday sign influences an individual's approach to situations. For instance, a cardinal sign birthday indicates an inclination towards initiating action and leadership.

Understanding both elements and modalities in the context of birthdays provides a comprehensive view of an individual's astrological profile, offering insights into their inherent characteristics and approach to life.

Numerology Integration

Numerology and Birthdays:

1. Life Path Number:

- *Calculation:* Sum of birthdate digits reduced to a single-digit (e.g., 25/07/1990 → 2+5+0+7+1+9+9+0 = 33 → 3+3 = 6).

- *Significance:* Reveals the overarching life journey and core personality traits.

2. Expression Number:

- *Calculation:* Assign numerical values to each letter in the full birth name, then sum and reduce to a single digit.

- *Significance:* Reflects how one expresses themselves and their abilities.

3. Soul Urge Number:

- *Calculation:* Assign numerical values to the vowels in the full birth name, then sum and reduce.

- *Significance:* Represents inner desires, motivations, and the true self.

4. Personality Number:

- *Calculation:* Assign numerical values to the consonants in the full birth name, then sum and reduce.

• *Significance:* Describes the outward personality and how one is perceived by others.

Integration Tips:
1. Combined Insights:

• Utilize both astrology and numerology to provide a holistic view of an individual's traits and tendencies.

2. Identify Patterns:

• Explore commonalities between astrological and numerological findings for a more nuanced analysis.

3. Highlight Uniqueness:

• Emphasize that each person's combination of astrological elements and numerological aspects is unique, contributing to their individuality.

4. Guidance for Growth:

• Use numerology to offer guidance on areas of personal development and potential challenges, complementing astrological insights.

Example Integration:
• A person with a fire sign (Aries), life path number 1 (independence and leadership), and expression number 5 (adventurous and freedom-loving) might embody a dynamic and pioneering spirit.

Final Note:
• Numerology enhances the astrological narrative, providing additional layers to the understanding of an individual's personality and life path.

Compatibility and Relationships

1. Sun Sign Compatibility:
- *Consideration:* Assess compatibility based on sun signs for general insights.
- *Insight:* Certain signs may naturally complement each other, while others may require understanding and compromise.

2. Moon Sign Harmony:
- *Consideration:* Examine moon sign compatibility for emotional connection.
- *Insight:* Compatible moon signs enhance emotional understanding and communication in relationships.

3. Venus and Mars Pairing:
- *Consideration:* Analyze the placement of Venus (love) and Mars (passion) in each partner's chart.
- *Insight:* Harmony in these placements fosters a balanced and fulfilling romantic connection.

4. Ascendant Influence:
- *Consideration:* Explore how the rising sign (ascendant) influences interpersonal dynamics.
- *Insight:* Similar ascendant signs may enhance compatibility in terms of communication and shared values.

5. Elements and Modalities:
- *Consideration:* Assess compatibility based on shared or complementary elements and modalities.
- *Insight:* Compatible elemental and modal influences contribute to a harmonious balance in the relationship.

6. Synastry Charts:
- *Consideration:* Examine synastry charts for a detailed comparison of both partners' astrological placements.

• *Insight:* Synastry charts provide a comprehensive view of strengths, challenges, and overall compatibility.

7. Timing of Transits:

• *Consideration:* Consider the timing of planetary transits in both partners' charts.

• *Insight:* Planetary transits can influence the dynamics of a relationship, indicating periods of growth or challenges.

Tips for Relationship Enhancement:

- **Communication:** Emphasize the importance of open and honest communication to navigate differences.
- **Understanding Differences:** Encourage acceptance of astrological differences and view them as opportunities for growth.
- **Shared Interests:** Identify shared interests and activities to strengthen the bond between partners.

Understanding astrological factors in relationships offers valuable insights into compatibility, communication styles, and potential areas of growth. It serves as a tool for fostering understanding and harmony in interpersonal connections.

Astrological Transits and Life Events

1. Overview of Planetary Transits:

• *Explanation:* Planetary transits occur as planets move through different positions in the sky relative to one's birth chart.

• *Impact:* These transits can influence various aspects of life, shaping experiences and events.

2. Personalized Timing:

• *Individual Influence:* The impact of transits is personalized, depending on the planets involved and their placement in the birth chart.

• *Timing Significance:* Understanding the timing of transits helps anticipate potential life changes.

3. Major Transits:

• *Saturn Return:* Occurs approximately every 29.5 years, signifying a transformative period in one's life, often involving career and identity reassessment.

• *Uranus Opposition:* Around age 42, brings a desire for change and self-discovery, often leading to shifts in personal and professional life.

4. Positive and Challenging Transits:

• *Jupiter Transit:* Brings opportunities for expansion and growth in various life areas.

• *Challenging Aspects:* Transits involving Saturn or Pluto may present challenges, prompting growth through adversity.

5. Career and Relationship Shifts:

• *Midheaven Transits:* Influence career changes and shifts in public life.

• *7th House Transits:* Affect partnerships and relationships, potentially leading to significant developments.

6. Emotional and Spiritual Growth:

- *Neptune Transits:* Inspire spiritual exploration and creativity but may also introduce illusions or confusion.
- *Pluto Transits:* Bring deep transformation, often involving internal growth and overcoming obstacles.

7. Navigating Transits:

- *Self-Reflection:* Encourage individuals to reflect on their birth chart and be aware of upcoming transits.
- *Adaptability:* Emphasize the importance of adaptability and openness during times of significant transits.

8. Seeking Guidance:

- *Consulting an Astrologer:* Suggest seeking guidance from an astrologer for a personalized interpretation of transits.
- *Self-Reflection Tools:* Promote journaling or self-reflection during key transit periods.

Understanding the influence of planetary transits provides individuals with insights into potential life events, allowing them to navigate transitions with greater awareness and preparedness.

Practical Applications of Astrological Insights

1. Self-Awareness and Personal Growth:

- *Daily Reflection:* Encourage individuals to reflect on their sun, moon, and rising signs regularly.
- *Goal:* Foster self-awareness, helping them understand their strengths, challenges, and areas for personal development.

2. Decision-Making:

- *Considering Transits:* Suggest checking current planetary transits before making significant decisions.
- *Purpose:* Align decision-making with favorable astrological influences for better outcomes.

3. Time Management:

- *Lunar Phases:* Align important activities with the lunar phases (new moon for new beginnings, full moon for culmination).
- *Outcome:* Enhance productivity and effectiveness by working in harmony with lunar energies.

4. Relationship Dynamics:

- *Synastry Analysis:* Explore synastry charts with partners to understand compatibility.
- *Benefit:* Improve communication and navigate relationship challenges with astrological insights.

5. Career Planning:

- *Midheaven Exploration:* Delve into the Midheaven sign and its aspects for insights into career preferences.
- *Advantage:* Align career choices with astrological strengths and inclinations.

6. Health and Well-Being:

- *Consideration of Ruling Planet:* Explore the ruling planet of one's sun sign for health-related insights.

• *Action:* Adopt lifestyle choices that resonate with the astrological qualities associated with the ruling planet.

7. Setting Intentions:

• *New Moon Rituals:* Encourage setting intentions during the new moon for manifestation.

• *Practice:* Engage in rituals that align with personal and professional goals.

8. Timing Events:

• *Electional Astrology:* Explore electional astrology for choosing auspicious times for significant events.

• *Outcome:* Optimize the likelihood of success and positive outcomes in various life events.

9. Daily Planning:

• *Daily Horoscope Check:* Incorporate a quick daily horoscope check to gain insights into daily energies.

• *Result:* Plan activities in alignment with astrological forecasts for a smoother day.

10. Mindful Living: - *Mindfulness Practices:* Integrate mindfulness practices with astrological insights for holistic well-being. - *Purpose:* Foster a balanced and harmonious lifestyle based on astrological principles.

Empowering individuals to apply astrological insights in their daily lives provides practical tools for better decision-making, self-understanding, and a more mindful approach to various aspects of life.

Astrological Case Studies

1. Empowering Career Shift (Aries Sun, Capricorn Rising):

* *Individual:* A person with Aries sun and Capricorn rising experienced a significant career shift during a Saturn return.

* *Observation:* The Saturn return prompted a reevaluation of career goals, leading to a bold decision to pursue a more challenging but fulfilling path.

* *Outcome:* The individual's leadership skills (Aries) and disciplined approach (Capricorn) synergized for a successful transition.

2. Relationship Dynamics (Libra Sun, Scorpio Moon):

* *Individual:* A couple with a Libra sun and Scorpio moon respectively sought relationship insights through synastry analysis.

* *Observation:* The compatibility of Libra's diplomatic nature with Scorpio's intensity was reflected in their communication styles.

* *Outcome:* Understanding each other's astrological influences enhanced their relationship dynamics, fostering deeper emotional connection.

3. Entrepreneurial Success (Leo Sun, Sagittarius Midheaven):

* *Individual:* An entrepreneur with a Leo sun and Sagittarius midheaven (MC) sought astrological guidance for business decisions.

* *Observation:* The individual's natural flair for creativity (Leo) aligned with the adventurous and visionary qualities of Sagittarius MC.

* *Outcome:* Strategic business decisions, aligned with favorable transits, contributed to the entrepreneur's success and recognition.

4. Health Consciousness (Virgo Sun, Taurus Ascendant):

* *Individual:* A health-conscious person with a Virgo sun and Taurus ascendant sought insights for holistic well-being.

• *Observation:* The Virgo sun's attention to detail paired with the Taurus ascendant's focus on physical well-being reflected in lifestyle choices.

• *Outcome:* Mindful alignment with the ruling planet Mercury (Virgo) and Venus (Taurus) contributed to a balanced and health-conscious lifestyle.

5. Creative Expression (Pisces Sun, Gemini Moon):

• *Individual:* A creative individual with a Pisces sun and Gemini moon explored the astrological aspects of their artistic journey.

• *Observation:* The dreamy and imaginative nature of Pisces sun complemented the versatile and communicative qualities of Gemini moon.

• *Outcome:* Understanding the astrological interplay empowered the individual to harness the synergy for enhanced creative expression.

6. Relationship Transformation (Scorpio Sun, Aquarius Venus):

• *Individual:* A person with a Scorpio sun and Aquarius Venus sought guidance during a challenging relationship phase.

• *Observation:* The deep emotional intensity of Scorpio sun intersected with the desire for independence and uniqueness in relationships (Aquarius Venus).

• *Outcome:* Astrological insights provided a framework for navigating challenges, fostering growth, and transforming the relationship positively.

These case studies illustrate the real-life impact of astrological influences on individuals, showcasing how awareness and understanding of astrological factors can guide decisions, enhance relationships, and contribute to personal growth.

February, the second month of the year, has a rich history and significance in various cultures and calendars. Let's delve into the origins and explore its multifaceted importance.

1. Roman Roots: In the ancient Roman calendar, February was originally the last month of the year. It had 28 days, except during leap years when an extra day was added. The name "February" is believed to derive from the Latin word "februum," meaning purification, as it was a time for cleansing rituals.

2. Februa Festival: The Romans celebrated the Februa festival during this month, a period of purification and atonement. This festival contributed to the association of February with cleansing and renewal.

3. Transition in Calendars: With the adoption of the Julian calendar by Julius Caesar in 45 BCE, February retained its place as the second month. The Gregorian calendar, introduced by Pope Gregory XIII in 1582 to align the calendar year with the solar year, further refined the leap year rules.

4. Celebrations in Honor of Deities: In ancient Rome, February was dedicated to the deities Juno and Lupercus. Juno was the goddess of marriage and women, and Lupercus was associated with shepherds and fertility. The Lupercalia festival, held in mid-February, involved rituals of purification and fertility.

5. Candlemas and Groundhog Day: February 2nd marks Candlemas, a Christian festival commemorating the presentation of Jesus at the Temple. Additionally, Groundhog Day, with its roots in European weather lore, falls on this date, symbolizing the midpoint between the winter solstice and the spring equinox.

6. Chinese New Year: In the lunar-based Chinese calendar, February hosts the celebration of the Chinese New Year. This vibrant festival, also known as the Spring Festival, marks the beginning of the lunar new year and is a time for family reunions, feasts, and cultural festivities.

7. Birthstone and Birth Flower: Amethyst, a purple gemstone symbolizing clarity and inner strength, is the birthstone for February. Additionally, the violet is the birth flower, representing modesty and faithfulness.

8. Modern Traditions: In contemporary times, February is celebrated with Valentine's Day on the 14th, a day dedicated to love and affection. It has become a month associated with matters of the heart and expressions of love.

9. Historical Birthdays: Some notable historical figures born in February include Abraham Lincoln, George Washington, Charles Darwin, and Rosa Parks, contributing to the month's significance in the annals of history.

In conclusion, February's history is woven with threads of ancient Roman rituals, Christian traditions, and diverse cultural celebrations. Its place in various calendars and its associations with purification, fertility, and love make it a month of layered significance across the ages.

Explore the science behind birthdays

including genetics, prenatal development, and the impact of birth order. Offer insights into potential influences without making deterministic claims.

The science behind birthdays encompasses a fascinating interplay of genetics, prenatal development, and birth order. While these factors contribute to shaping certain aspects of individuals, it's essential to acknowledge that they are not deterministic and that a wide range of influences shapes our personalities and traits.

1. **Genetics:**

   ○ **Inherited Traits:** Many aspects of our personalities and physical characteristics are influenced by our genetic makeup. Traits such as intelligence, temperament, and even susceptibility to certain health conditions can have a genetic component.

   ○ **Genetic Diversity:** The combination of genes inherited from our parents creates a unique genetic profile. However, genetic diversity is vast, and individuals with the same birthday can have widely varying characteristics.

2. **Prenatal Development:**

   ○ **Intrauterine Environment:** The environment in the womb during prenatal development can play a role in shaping certain characteristics. Factors such as maternal nutrition, stress levels, and exposure to substances can influence fetal development.

   ○ **Epigenetics:** Epigenetic factors, which involve changes in gene expression without altering the underlying DNA sequence, can be influenced by environmental factors during pregnancy.

3. Birth Order:

○ **Sibling Dynamics:** Birth order, or the order in which siblings are born, can influence personality traits. First-borns, middle children, and youngest siblings may develop different characteristics based on their unique family dynamics.

○ **Parental Expectations:** Parents often have different expectations and parenting styles for their first, middle, or last-born children, which can contribute to the development of certain traits.

4. Environmental Factors:

○ **Cultural and Social Influences:** The cultural and social environment in which individuals are raised can have a profound impact on their development. Cultural norms, societal expectations, and economic conditions contribute to the diversity of personalities.

○ **Educational and Experiential Factors:** The educational experiences and life events individuals encounter shape their perspectives and skills. These factors contribute significantly to the diverse array of personalities.

5. Personality Psychology:

○ **The Big Five Traits:** Personality traits, as identified in the Big Five model (openness, conscientiousness, extraversion, agreeableness, and neuroticism), are complex and influenced by a combination of genetic and environmental factors.

○ **Individual Differences:** While there may be general trends associated with certain birth months or birth orders, individual differences within groups are substantial. People born on the same day or in the same position in a family can have remarkably different personalities.

In conclusion, the science behind birthdays involves a complex interplay of genetic factors, prenatal influences, birth order dynamics, and environmental conditions. It's crucial to appreciate the vast range of influences and understand that individual differences play a significant role in shaping each person's unique characteristics. While certain trends may exist, the diversity of human experiences ensures that each individual is a product of a multifaceted and intricate interplay of factors.

Unique Traditions and Festivities

For February Birthdays Around the World:

Europe:

● Candlemas (February 2nd): Celebrated in many European countries, Candlemas involves blessing candles and parading them through the streets. It signifies the halfway point between winter solstice and spring equinox, symbolizing hope and the return of light.

● Carnival: February is prime carnival season in various European countries like Italy, France, and Spain. Filled with vibrant costumes, parades, and revelry, it marks the last hurrah before the somber Lent period.

● Lappland, Finland: In Finnish Lapland, February is the month of the Hibernation Games, where locals compete in unusual winter sports like wife-carrying and reindeer racing.

Asia:

● Setsubun (February 3rd): A Japanese festival marking the beginning of spring, Setsubun involves throwing roasted soybeans from houses to ward off evil spirits and bring good luck.

● Lunar New Year: Celebrated in China, Vietnam, Korea, and other Asian countries, Lunar New Year falls sometime in February and involves family reunions, traditional meals, and lion dances.

● Tibetan Losar: Celebrated in February or March, Tibetan Losar marks the Tibetan New Year with colorful prayer flags, yak butter lamp offerings, and traditional dances.

Africa:

● Yaoundé Carnival, Cameroon: Held in February, this vibrant carnival boasts elaborate costumes, music, and dance, showcasing Cameroon's rich cultural heritage.

● Enkutatash, Ethiopia: Celebrated on January 7th (Ethiopian calendar), Enkutatash signifies the birth of Jesus and features colorful processions, feasts, and bonfires.

● Mbongeni Festival, Swaziland: Held in February or March, Mbongeni celebrates the King's birthday with traditional dances, music, and cattle displays.

Americas:

● Groundhog Day (February 2nd): In North America, Groundhog Day predicts the end of winter. If the groundhog sees its shadow, six more weeks of winter are expected.

● Mardi Gras (Shrove Tuesday, before Lent): Celebrated in New Orleans and other parts of the US, Mardi Gras involves elaborate parades, costumes, and music, culminating in Fat Tuesday's revelry.

● Carnival in Rio de Janeiro, Brazil: This world-famous carnival, held in February or March, features stunning samba dancers, extravagant costumes, and pulsating music, showcasing Brazil's vibrant culture.

Folklore and Superstitions:

● February babies are said to be strong, independent, and adaptable, possibly due to enduring the coldest months.

● The February birthstone, amethyst, is believed to bring good luck, protection, and inner peace.

● In some cultures, February is considered an unlucky month for weddings or starting new ventures.

Remember, these are just a few examples, and many more unique traditions and superstitions exist around the world. You can research specific cultures or regions to discover fascinating insights into how people celebrate February birthdays.

February Birthday Celebrations: Unleash the Inner Flame!

February's birthdays, nestled between winter's chill and spring's promise, deserve celebrations as unique and captivating as the month itself. Let's ditch the generic cake and explore personalized ways to make a February birthday truly meaningful and memorable.

Unleashing Individuality:

• Tap into Passions: Is the birthday star an avid bookworm? Surprise them with a cozy literary-themed party, book swap, or author meet-and-greet. For the foodie, curate a progressive gourmet dinner around their favorite cuisines. If music fuels their soul, throw a themed karaoke bash or organize a private acoustic set by their local favorites.

• Embrace Winter Wonder: Channel the crisp February air with an outdoor ice skating or stargazing party. Plan a cozy bonfire gathering with hot drinks and shared stories. Turn it into a winter sports extravaganza with sledding, ice fishing, or even a DIY snowman building competition.

• Creative Pursuits: For the artistic soul, organize a pottery painting or jewelry-making workshop. If nature beckons, embark on a guided hike or scenic photography expedition. Unleash inner talents with a paint and sip party or a DIY craft workshop focused on the birthday person's favorite hobby.

Meaningful Touches:

• Personalized Gifts: Go beyond the store-bought and create something bespoke. Craft a heartfelt scrapbook filled with memories and well-wishes from loved ones. Compose a personalized poem or song that captures their essence. Bake their favorite childhood cake or whip up a gourmet dish inspired by their culinary dreams.

• Acts of Service: Show you care through actions. Offer to help them with a long-held project, volunteer together for a cause they champion, or surprise them by cleaning their apartment and preparing a romantic candlelit dinner.

• Experience over Things: Gift memories that last a lifetime. Book tickets to a concert by their favorite artist, organize a weekend getaway to a cozy cabin, or plan a surprise outing to a hidden local gem they've always wanted to visit.

Celebrating with Style:

• Themed Decorations: Transform your space into a winter wonderland with fairy lights, snow-laden branches, and cozy blankets. For a festive flair, embrace Carnival vibes with vibrant decorations, masks, and feathers. Or, channel an ancient Roman theme with laurel wreaths, draped fabric, and DIY clay lamps.

• Personalized Soundtrack: Curate a playlist filled with the birthday person's favorite songs, nostalgic tunes, and hidden gems that reflect their personality. Let the music set the mood and add a touch of personal magic to the celebration.

• Interactive Games: Ditch the generic party games and create some laughter-filled activities unique to the birthday theme. For a literary party, hold a trivia night based on their favorite books, or for a winter wonderland theme, organize a scavenger hunt for hidden winter treats.

Remember, the best February birthday celebrations are those that tap into the individual's passions, offer meaningful connections, and create lasting memories. So, be creative, embrace the unique charm of February, and let the festivities ignite the inner flame of the birthday star!

February Birthdays:

Blossoming Between Frost and Bloom

February, a month often painted in cold strokes, holds a hidden warmth for those born under its icy stars. It whispers of resilience, cradles new beginnings, and bursts with potential waiting to bloom. Let's weave a tapestry of words to celebrate February birthdays, uplifting spirits and adding a touch of sentimentality to their journey.

Inspirational Quotes:

● "You don't choose your birthday. You get handed it like a gift. All you can do is decide what to do with it." - Katherine Hepburn, a vibrant February spirit who embodied life's possibilities.

● "Spring will not break if you don't let it. But love can bloom anytime, for as long as you are a living soul." - Rumi, a reminder that February's chill cannot quench the fire of a hopeful heart.

● "And remember, even the darkest night will end with the rising of the sun." - Victor Hugo, a beacon of optimism for when doubt creeps in during February's coldest days.

Poems for Renewal:

Frost Kissed Bloom:

Beneath the frost, a seed takes root, In February's heart, whispers of fruit. Though winter lingers, icy and gray, Hope's embers glow, waiting for spring's play.

From frozen ground, a shoot will rise, Unfurling green against the clear skies. Sunlight's caress, a tender touch, Awakens buds, promising so much.

So raise a glass to February's might, Where darkness yields to dawning light. For in this month, where resilience thrives, New beginnings bloom, and life survives.

Stories of Transformation:

The tale of the Snow Queen, trapped in perpetual winter, can serve as a cautionary tale, reminding us to keep the fires of hope and passion burning bright, even in February's harshest moments.

For a lighter touch, share the myth of Persephone, who descends into the underworld during winter only to return to the earth reborn and radiant, symbolizing the inevitable renewal that follows even the darkest times.

Conclusion: Embrace the Cosmic Tapestry of Self-Discovery

In the journey of self-discovery, astrology offers a captivating lens through which individuals can understand the intricacies of their personalities, relationships, and life events. Here are key takeaways:

1. Unveiling Personal Blueprint:

- Astrology, with its elements, modalities, and planetary influences, unveils a unique cosmic blueprint for each person.

- Understanding sun, moon, and rising signs provides foundational insights into character, emotions, and outward demeanor.

2. Navigating Life Events:

- Planetary transits mark significant periods of transformation, growth, and challenges in one's life.

- By aligning with favorable transits, individuals can navigate life events with awareness and purpose.

3. Interpersonal Dynamics:

- Astrological insights contribute to understanding relationship dynamics through synastry, fostering better communication and compatibility.

- Recognizing the astrological influences on partnerships enhances empathy and connection.

4. Practical Applications:

- Daily application of astrological insights empowers decision-making, time management, and overall well-being.

- Incorporating astrology in various aspects of life aligns actions with cosmic energies for optimal results.

5. Case Studies Illuminate Real-Life Impact:

- Real-life examples showcase how individuals, armed with astrological awareness, navigate career shifts, enhance relationships, and achieve entrepreneurial success.

- The synergy of astrological elements shapes diverse paths, each uniquely contributing to personal growth.

6. Encouragement for Self-Reflection:

- Embrace astrology as a tool for self-reflection, self-awareness, and continuous growth.

- The cosmic tapestry of astrological influences invites individuals to explore, understand, and celebrate their authentic selves.

As you embark on this cosmic exploration, may the wisdom of the stars guide you toward a deeper understanding of yourself and those around you. Embrace the dynamic interplay of celestial forces, and may your journey be filled with self-discovery, empowerment, and a harmonious alignment with the cosmic rhythms of life.

Remember, in the dance of the cosmos, your unique steps shape a story that is yours to unfold.

Contact the astrologer

We extend our sincere thanks to you, dear readers, for embarking on this astrological journey with us. Your curiosity, engagement, and trust have made this exploration of the Zodiac sign Cancer all the more fulfilling.

In these pages, we have delved into the essence of the Cancer sign, unveiling its secrets, traits, and the horoscope for 2024. We've ventured through the depths of emotion, explored the intricacies of relationships, and discovered the likes and dislikes of a Cancer individual. All of this would not have been possible without your interest and presence.

Your quest for knowledge and self-discovery is what fuels our passion for astrology, and we are grateful to have been your guides in this cosmic voyage. We hope that the insights and wisdom shared in these pages serve as a guiding light in your life.

We invite you to explore our other books, each dedicated to a unique Zodiac sign and various aspects of astrology. Whether you seek to deepen your understanding of the stars or uncover the mysteries of other signs, you'll find a wealth of knowledge waiting for you.

Should you have any questions, insights, or simply wish to connect with us, please don't hesitate to reach out.

You can contact us via

WhatsApp at +1829-205-5456

or

email us at danielsanjurjo47@gmail.com.

May the stars continue to shine brightly on your path, and may your journey through the Zodiac signs be filled with enlightenment, growth, and harmony. **Sincerely Daniel Sanjurjo**

Embracing Cosmic Wisdom: A Journey Through "The Secret Language of Birthdays - February Profiles: Personality Insights"

Hey fellow cosmic explorers! As we wrap up our adventure with "The Secret Language of Birthdays - February Profiles: Personality Insights," take a moment to soak in the celestial wisdom it's gifted you. Thanks to the stellar guidance of Daniel Sanjurjo and his fantastic team, you're now equipped with more than just zodiac tidbits – you've got a cosmic key to understanding your very essence.

This book isn't just about ruling planets and lucky colors; it's a cosmic roadmap to self-discovery. So, as we close this chapter, remember that your journey doesn't end here. Daniel Sanjurjo has an entire constellation of astrology books waiting for you. Each one opens up a universe of insights and revelations about the cosmic dance above.

Feeling thirsty for more cosmic knowledge? Well, good news! Dive into other works by Sanjurjo; there's a whole cosmic library waiting to unveil the mysteries written in the stars.

About the Author

Daniel Sanjurjo is a passionate author who delves into the realms of astrology and self-help. With a gift for exploring the celestial and the human psyche, Daniel's books are celestial journeys of self-discovery and personal growth. Join the cosmic odyssey with this insightful writer.

Don't miss out!

Visit the website below and you can sign up to receive emails whenever Daniel Sanjurjo publishes a new book. There's no charge and no obligation.

https://books2read.com/r/B-A-WQHBB-HYQSC

BOOKS2READ

Connecting independent readers to independent writers.

Did you love *The Secret Language of Birthdays - February Personality Insights*? Then you should read *Aquarius 2024*[1] by Daniel Sanjurjo!

Aquarius, 2024: Your Cosmic Guide to a Year of Transformation!

Attention Aquarius Enthusiasts!

Embark on a celestial journey like never before with "Aquarius 2024," your go-to guide for navigating the cosmic currents. This insightful monthly horoscope is tailored specifically for Aquarius individuals, providing a personalized and immersive experience that unveils the mysteries of each month in 2024.

Yearning for a deeper connection with the cosmos? "Aquarius 2024" fulfills your desire for in-depth insights. Delve into the details of each month, uncovering the secrets that the stars have in store for you.

---

1. https://books2read.com/u/b5BZBw

2. https://books2read.com/u/b5BZBw

Take action and seize the opportunities that align with your cosmic energy. Whether it's navigating challenges, fostering relationships, or achieving financial success, this guide empowers you to make the most of every cosmic alignment.

What to Expect:

Detailed Monthly Forecasts: Explore love, family, marriage, financial prospects, work, health, and interactions with siblings and children in each monthly section.

In-Depth Insights: Uncover the significance of celestial events and their impact on your life. From the influence of planets to the energy of the moon, understand how cosmic forces shape your journey.

Practical Guidance: Receive practical advice on how to navigate challenges and leverage opportunities. The guide is tailored to assist you in making informed decisions in various aspects of your life.

Engaging Writing Style: Written in a conversational and approachable tone, "Aquarius 2024" ensures an enjoyable reading experience, making the complexities of astrology easy to understand.

Embark on a transformative journey with "Aquarius 2024," your companion through the cosmic currents of the upcoming year. Whether you're an astrology enthusiast or just curious about what the stars have in store, this guide is your key to unlocking the secrets of 2024. Don't miss the chance to make this year truly cosmic!

Also by Daniel Sanjurjo

Birthdays Profiles
The Secret Language of Birthdays Profiles - January Personality Insights.
The Secret Language of Birthdays - February Personality Insights

Zodiaco
Aries 2024 Mes Por Mes
Tauro 2024 Mes Por Mes
Géminis 2024 Mes Por Mes
Cáncer 2024 Mes Por Mes
Leo 2024 Mes Por Mes:
Virgo 2024 Mes Por Mes
Libra 2024 Mes Por Mes
Escorpio 2024 Mes Por Mes
Sagitario 2024 Mes Por Mes
Capricornio 2024 Mes Por Mes
Acuario 2024 Mes Por Mes
Piscis 2024: Un Viaje Celestial
Piscis 2024 Mes Por Mes

Zodiac world
Aries Revealed 2024
Taurus 2024
Leo 2024
Gemini 2024
Cancer horoscope 2024
Virgo 2024
Scorpio 2024
Sagittarius 2024
Capricorn 2024
Aquarius 2024

Standalone
Cosmic Revelations 2024
Dreams Interpretation Guide
Explorando Mis Sueños: Descubre el Mundo Fascinante de tu Mente Nocturna